COLORFUL
Machine
Knitting Patterns

Sterling Publishing Co., Inc.   New York

Library of Congress Cataloging-in-Publication Data

Harmony guide to colourful machine knitting
    Colorful machine knitting patterns.
        p.   cm.
    Originally published: The Harmony guide to colourful machine
knitting. Great Britain : Lyric Books, © 1989.
    ISBN 0-8069-8464-3
    1. Knitting, Machine—Patterns.   I. Title.
TT680.H35   1991
746.9'2—dc20   91-13265
                                                          CIP

Compiled by Barbara Devaney

10 9 8 7 6 5 4 3 2 1

Published in North America in 1991 by
Sterling Publishing Company, Inc.
387 Park Avenue South, New York, N.Y. 10016
Originally published in Great Britain under the
title *The Harmony Guide to Colourful Machine Knitting*
© 1989 by Lyric Books Limited
Distributed in Canada by Sterling Publishing
% Canadian Manda Group, P.O. Box 920, Station U
Toronto, Ontario, Canada M8Z 5P9
Printed and bound in Belgium
All rights reserved

Sterling ISBN 0-8069-8464-3

CONTENTS

Introduction

Colour is of supreme importance when creating fabrics. By using a knitting machine many exciting colourful fabrics can be produced. Effects that take much time and effort to knit by hand can quickly and easily be produced on a machine. The diagrams and charts on the following pages should inspire all standards of machine knitter and encourage you to explore the full potential of your machines.

Machines

All knitting machines have a bed of needles which produce stocking stitch and an infinite variety of stocking stitch variations. Many machines nowadays have facilities that enable them to produce patterns automatically. The most common method of automatic patterning is the 24 stitch punchcard but electronic methods (because of their greater flexibility) are also becoming popular.

The diagrams on the following pages have been designed with these methods in mind. The punchcard diagrams can all be transferred directly onto the pattern sheets used with electronic machines. Some of the electronic designs can be adapted for use with 24 stitch punchcard machines. Intarsia charts can be used with most knitting machines. It is also possible to reproduce most of the punchcard and electronic designs manually on any machine.

Gauge

Most 24 stitch punchcard and electronic machines are standard gauge. They work best using 4 ply yarn for motif and intarsia work, but will also knit finer and some slightly thicker yarns. The samples shown have been knitted using 4 ply wool yarn on a standard gauge machine. A different effect can be achieved by using a chunky gauge machine with large needles and thicker yarn.

Yarn

It is very important to prepare yarn before knitting. Irregular stitches can result from yarn that has not been adequately prepared. Ideally it should be wound onto a cone or into a ball using a mechanical ball winder. A commercially wound ball of yarn can be used so long as the end is taken from the centre and it is placed in a jar or box to prevent it rolling around.

The more hairy yarns should also be waxed to enable the carriage to run freely. Paraffin wax, available from machine stockists or a candle can be held against the yarn whilst it is being wound. Alternatively some machines have a place to hold wax so that the yarn automatically comes into contact with it before passing to the carriage. Any wax remaining on the finished knitted fabric can be removed with the first wash.

Most standard knitting machines work best when using a smooth, fine yarn. The chunky machines can handle a wider variety of yarn. However, it is possible to knit more hairy or fancy yarns of the correct thickness on standard gauge machines although care must be taken that they do not catch on the sinker posts. To check for caught loops run your fingers across the back of the knitting. A gentle downward tug of the work should release them. The more obstinate ones can be released using a latch tool. Do not be discouraged from using the more fancy yarns as they can give added interest to fabrics. For instance, try using a hairy or fancy yarn as the contrast colour in a 2-colour fair-isle or motif.

Tension / Gauge

It is essential when knitting a garment either from a commercial design or a design of your own to check tension/gauge. This is done by knitting swatches in the yarn or yarns to be used for the garment.

Cast on about 60 sts and knit about 20 cms [8 ins] (refer to your machine handbook for suggested tension dial number). The knitting must then be allowed to relax completely. If the yarn used is a wool or wool/synthetic mixture it will help the yarn to relax if it is steamed thoroughly without allowing the weight of the iron to rest on the work. If the yarn is predominantly synthetic ease the work in with your fingers and allow it to rest for as long as possible.

If you are working from a commercial design, mark with pins the number of stitches and rows as stated in the instructions to give 10 cms [4 ins] square (see below). If this does not measure exactly 10 cms [4 ins] square, work another tension piece tighter (if the piece is too large) or looser (if the piece is too small). Continue in this way until you find the correct tension.

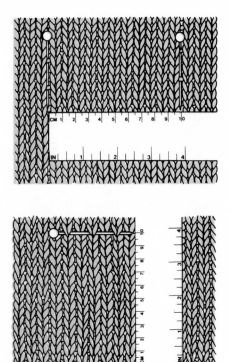

Consult your machine handbook for alternative methods of checking tension/guage.

If you are going to use a diagram or chart from this book to design a garment of your own continue testing until you have a sample that is at a suitable tension (neither too stiff nor too floppy).

This may seem to be a long, complicated procedure but with time it should become automatic. Care taken at this initial stage will avoid time wasted and the disappointment that will result if the finished garment is unsatisfactory.

Formation of Stocking Stitch

Stocking stitch is the basic fabric produced on domestic machines and a knowledge of how it is formed will help you to prevent and rectify mistakes. When working in stocking stitch the purl side is facing you and the knit side is away from you. Generally, fairisle fabrics and fabrics with motifs or areas of intarsia use the knit side as the right side of the work. The main parts of the knitting machine are the needle bed which holds the individual latch needles and the knit carriage that can slide across the needle bed.

The carriage controls the movement of the latch needles.

The Latch Needle

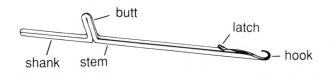

There are four basic needle positions and these positions are usually marked by letters or numbers at the sides of the needle bed.

Needle Positions

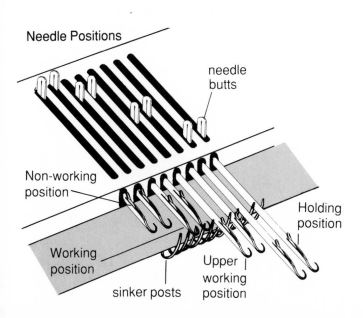

In the Non-Working Position the needles cannot be used for knitting. They will not move when the carriage passes over them. The needles have to be brought forward to Working Position in order to knit. Stitches can be made to 'hold' on needles in holding position until released. Consult your manual to find out how to do this. Your manual will give a more detailed description of the needle positions which can vary slightly from model to model.

Formation of an Individual Stitch

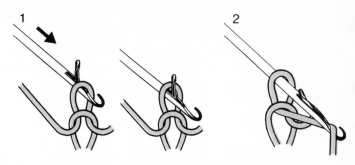

1. As the needle is moved forward, the stitch moves back, opening the latch and slipping behind it.

2. The carriage moves across the needle laying yarn in the open latch.

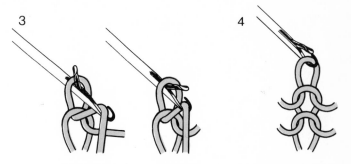

3. The needle then moves back, the old stitch moves forward and closes the latch over the yarn in the hook.

4. The needle returns to Working Position, the old stitch slides over the latch and off the needle. The yarn laid in the hook is pulled through to form a new stitch.

The best way to see the action of the latch needle is to move it by hand. Once you are familiar with the way stitches are formed it should be much easier to pick up and knit dropped stitches with the latch tool. Also, half-knitted rows caused by the carriage jamming should no longer be a problem as they can be finished off by hand.

The Latch Tool

Methods of Cast On

Open Edge Cast On

This method is quick and simple but it produces an unfinished edge that will unravel making it ideal for tension, or test pieces. It can also be used for garment pieces that have to be grafted together or where the edge is subsequently hooked back onto the needles to make a hem. In this case waste yarn should be used for cast on and to knit several rows before changing to main yarn.

1. Push forward required number of needles to Working Position.

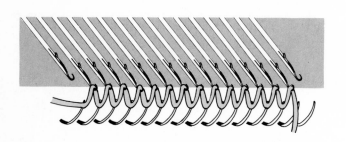

2. With yarn in the feeder, move carriage across the needle bed once. The yarn should be caught alternately between sinker posts and needles. It is important that all the needles return to Working Position with no uneven loops at the edge.

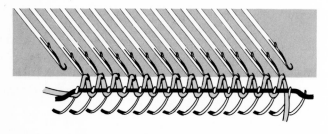

3. Lay a nylon cord (available from machine stockists) across the loops as shown.

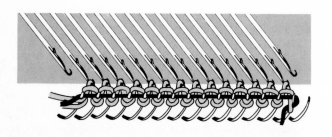

4. Holding both ends of the nylon cord pull it down firmly and move the carriage across the needle bed slowly. Knit 3 or 4 rows before releasing nylon cord. Cast on is complete.

Closed Edge Cast On

This method produces a finished edge that does not unravel.

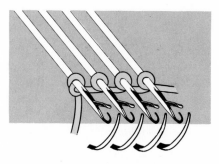

1. With carriage at right push forward required number of needles to Holding Position.

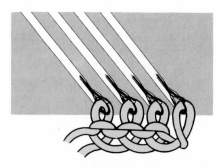

2. Fasten yarn to left end needle and loop it in an anti-clockwise direction around each needle. It is important to make the loops even. Push loops back to the stems of the needle behind the latch.

3. Thread the yarn into feeder, taking up any slack by hand. Move the carriage across the needle bed slowly. Return needles to Holding Position for the first 2 to 4 rows of knitting.

Increasing

To increase one stitch at edge of knitting simply move one needle forward into Working Position.

When the carriage is moved across the needle bed the empty needle will pick up the yarn.

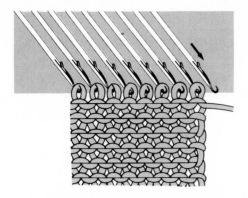

To increase several stitches on the carriage side push the needles to be increased into holding position. Wind the yarn around needles as for the closed edge. Take up slack yarn by hand and move carriage across needle bed slowly. Return needles to Holding Position for the first 2 to 4 rows of knitting.

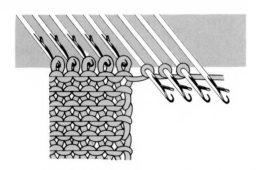

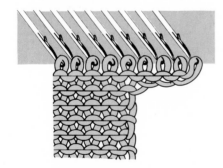

Methods Of Cast Off

Open Edge Cast Off

This method is quick and simple but it produces an unfinished edge that will unravel making it ideal for tension pieces. By changing to waste yarn several rows before casting off it can be used for garment pieces that have to be grafted together or where two pieces can be hooked onto the needles and cast off together (see Closed Edge Cast Off).

Remove yarn from feeder and move carriage across needle bed. Knitting will then drop from machine. For this reason care must be taken that yarn does not get accidentally removed from the feeder during knitting.

Closed Edge Cast Off

This method produces a finished edge that does not unravel.

The Transfer Tool

1. Using transfer tool, transfer end stitch nearest carriage to adjacent needle. Push this needle forward to Holding Position. Return empty needle to Non-Working Position.

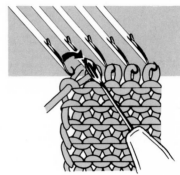

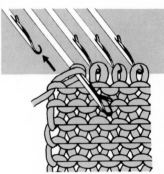

2. Lay yarn into the empty hook.

3. Hold yarn down and push the needle back to Working Position. The 2 stitches will slip off the needle, leaving a new stitch.

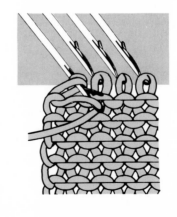

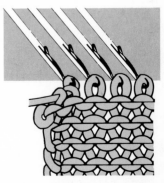

4. Continue the same procedure until left with one stitch. Break yarn and draw through remaining stitch to fasten off.

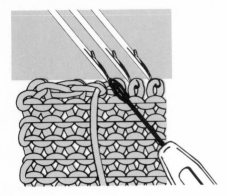

Decreasing

To decrease 1 stitch at edge of knitting simply transfer stitch to adjacent needle using transfer tool. Return empty needle to Non-Working Position before passing carriage over needle bed.

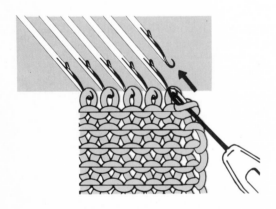

To decrease several stitches, finish with carriage on side where stitches are to be decreased. Decrease the required number of stitches using the same method as for a Closed Edge Cast Off.

Steaming

Most yarns benefit from steaming as this will allow the fabric to relax after being stretched on the machine. The steam draws the bars between the stitches into the stitches themselves and consequently the knitting contracts.

As a general guide, wool, cotton, linen and other natural yarns can be steam pressed but care should be taken with synthetic yarns. If synthetic fabrics are pressed too heavily no amount of washing will correct the resulting lifeless appearance of the fabric, therefore it is best to consult manufacturers' instructions or press a test piece first.

Blocking

Fabrics knitted in yarns that can be steamed are suitable for 'blocking'. This process flattens wavy fabric and 'fixes' the stitches.

1. With wrong side facing pin out each piece to the correct size and shape on a padded surface. Do not pin out ribs and welts as this will cause them to lose their elasticity.

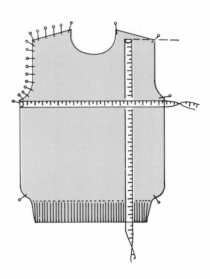

2. Lay a damp cloth over the work, then steam thoroughly. The heat from the steam is usually sufficient to shrink and set the fabric so it is not necessary to press the iron onto the fabric. Leave to dry before unpinning.

Joining and Finishing
Grafting

Two pieces of knitting that have 'Open Edges' can be joined invisibly by grafting.

1. Lay the pieces to be joined close together, with the stitches on each side corresponding to those opposite. Thread a wool or tapestry needle with the knitting yarn and pass it up through the right end stitch of the lower piece.

2. Pass the needle up through the first stitch of the upper piece.

1   2

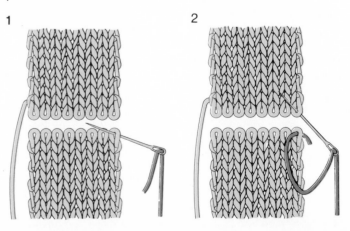

3. Pass it down through the first stitch of the lower piece then bring it up through the next stitch to the left.

4. Pass it down through the first stitch of the upper piece then bring it up through the next stitch to the left.

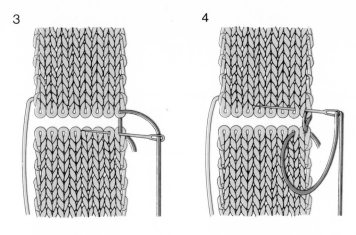

3   4

5. Repeat steps 3 and 4 with 2nd, 3rd and subsequent stitches.

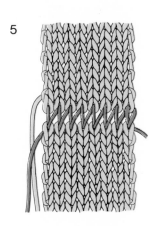

5

Mattress Stitch Seam

This type of seam gives the neatest, most professional finish.

1. Lay the pieces to be joined close together, with the stitches on each side corresponding to those opposite. Thread a wool or tapestry needle with the knitting yarn. Pass the needle under the top two bars on the right side.

2. Repeat this on the left side.

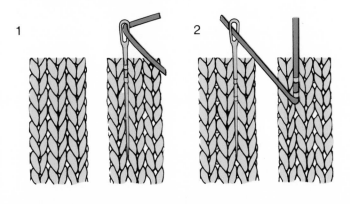

1   2

3. Return to the first side and pass the thread under the next two bars, repeating this first on one side and then on the other until a few stitches have been worked.

4. Pull the thread firmly so that the stitches are held together quite tightly. Stretch the seam slightly to give the required amount of elasticity, then continue with the next section of the seam.

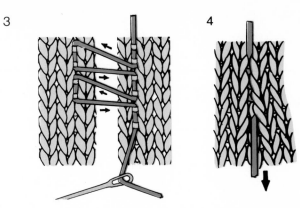

3   4

Mattress stitch can be worked either one stitch in from the edge as in the diagrams, or half a stitch in from the edge according to how neat the edge of the fabric is and how thick the yarn is. Where the knit side of the work is the right side, work under two rows (bars) at a time as shown. Where purl is used as the right side it is better to work under only one row (bar) at a time.

One advantage of mattress stitch is that it can be used to sew shaped edges together quite easily; because you are working on the right side of the work all the time it is much easier to see where you are and to keep the seam neat.

Punchcards

Punchcards are used to programme the machine for patterning. The holes and blanks on the cards determine which needles are selected to knit pattern stitches. The punchcard diagrams on the following pages have been designed specifically for machines that use punchcards with a maximum repeat of 24 stitches. However, they can be adapted for use with models that have a different maximum repeat.

The pattern area of the punchcard can be transferred directly onto an electronic chart for use with electronic machines. The 'holes' on the punchcard diagrams correspond to filled in squares on electronic charts. It is not always necessary to transfer the whole punchcard diagram onto an electronic chart because only one pattern repeat is needed to programme electronic machines. As an example the diagram of a punchcard shown on page 10 has one pattern repeat shaded. If you are unsure about doing this for yourself on any particular diagram simply transfer the whole punchcard diagram onto the electronic chart.

The patterns can be worked on non-automatic machines by hand selecting needles across the entire width of the fabric. Guide holes should be ignored when hand selecting needles for patterning.

To make your own pattern cards you will need blank punchcards and a hand punch, available from machine stockists.

The holes to be punched should be marked first with pencil. All punchcards should start and finish with 2 rows of guide holes as shown. These enable the card to be clipped together without obscuring any of the pattern. Care should be taken to punch the cards exactly as shown. If a mistake is made fill the punched hole with a piece of punched card and fix with adhesive tape being careful not to obscure any of the correct holes.

Once the punchcard has been made it will be easier to use if the row numbers are marked on it. Refer to the manual to discover how to number the card so that when row 1 is shown, the row being knitted corresponds with the bottom row of the diagram. It is important to start knitting at row 1 when following the colour changes given at the side of the diagrams. See your machine handbook for details of **your** machine.

Punchcard

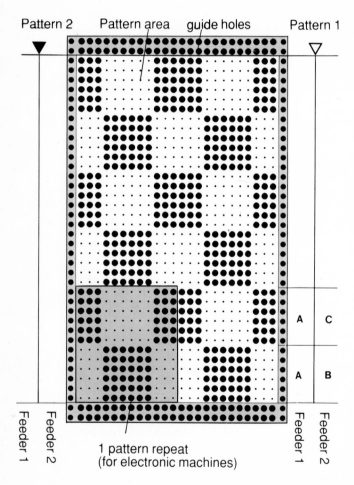

Pattern 2   Pattern area   guide holes   Pattern 1

A   C

A   B

Feeder 1   Feeder 2

1 pattern repeat
(for electronic machines)

Feeder 1   Feeder 2

Electronic Charts

Electronic charts are more versatile than punchcards at programming machines. The pattern area does not have to be a multiple that fits into 24 stitches and can be much larger than 24 stitches. Patterns and Motifs can be doubled in width and/or length and it is also possible to reverse designs. The coloured and non-coloured squares determine which needles are selected to knit pattern stitches.

Several of the electronic charts can be easily adapted for use with a 24 stitch punchcard machine. Where this is possible co-ordinates are given for the area that should be transferred to the punchcard. More than one punchcard can be clipped together for longer designs.

The patterns can be worked on non-automatic machines by hand selecting needles across the entire width of the fabric.

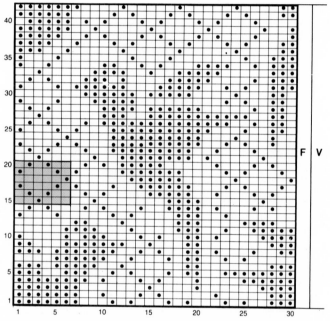

F   V

How to Read Punchcard Diagrams

To knit the fairisle sample shown, set the card to start knitting at row 1 and set the machine to knit fairisle. Place A in feeder 1 and B in feeder 2. Knit 6 rows. A remains in feeder 1, place C in feeder 2. Knit 6 rows. Repeat these 12 rows.

If there is no yarn shown in a feeder leave it empty to knit the required number of rows.

Where two patterns have been knitted using one punchcard, triangle symbols have been used to indicate the colourway that corresponds with the pattern.

How to Read Electronic Charts

The charts have all been numbered as if they have been placed on the bottom left-hand corner of an electronic programming chart. The co-ordinates indicating the pattern area are all given in the order (Bottom, Top, Left Side, Right Side). Thus the example shown has a pattern area determined by the co-ordinates (1,42,1,30). A second design can be obtained from the chart by programming the pattern area determined by the co-ordinates (15,20,1,6).

In order to utilise the whole electronic chart, the designs can be placed anywhere on it and the co-ordinates determining the pattern area will also change accordingly.

Colour changes have been indicated in the same way as for punchcard diagrams (see sections on Punchcards and How To Read Punchcard Diagrams). It is important to start knitting at Row 1 when following the colour changes given at the side of the diagrams. Where more than one sample has been knitted using the same chart, colour changes are given separately.

Colour Chart

The colours shown are approximate equivalents to yarn colours used in samples.

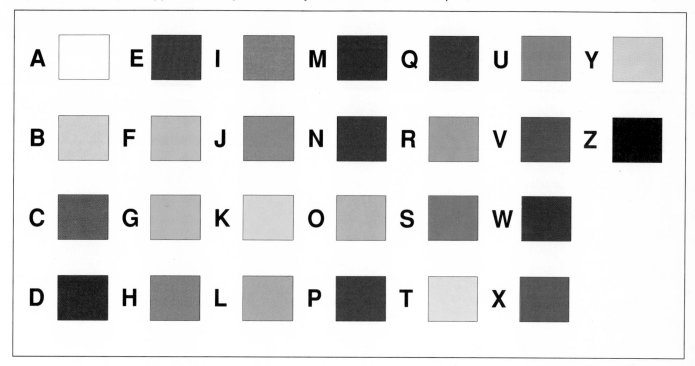

Colour

Diagrams include suggested colours and these have been indicated by a letter shown on the colour chart shown above.

As colour choice is so personal, do experiment yourself with colour combinations. A design knitted in bold contrast colours will look entirely different if soft muted colours are used. Why not try making use of pleasing colour combinations already in existence. A favourite scarf, rug or set of curtains can all provide inspiration. Having chosen a design it is well worth knitting samples in several colour combinations before commencing a garment.

Fairisle

Fairisle is a technique for producing stocking stitch fabric where two colours are used in the same row. One set of needles corresponding to the blank spaces on the diagrams knit the yarn in feeder 1. The second set of needles corresponding to the marked areas on the diagrams knit the yarn in feeder 2.

On non-automatic machines selected needles usually knit the yarn in feeder 2. Consult your machine manual to confirm the method for your machine. Needles corresponding to the marked areas on the diagrams should be selected across the entire width of the fabric. You may find it helpful to place a ruler underneath the row you are working on the diagrams.

On machines that have an end needle selector mechanism ensure that it is not in use when knitting rows that consist of only one colour within a fairisle pattern. (It will cause the 2nd colour to knit the first and last stitches only thus giving a float across the entire width of the fabric).

Patterns with more than 2 colours

To prevent cutting and rejoining yarn continuously do not thread the extra colours through the top tension discs of the machine. Keep the yarn at the side of the machine and feed it by hand.

Floats

The yarn not in use makes a 'float' across the back of the work. Long floats can cause problems in knitted fabric that is not lined. It is therefore best not to have too many stitches in the same colour together along one row of fairisle knitting.

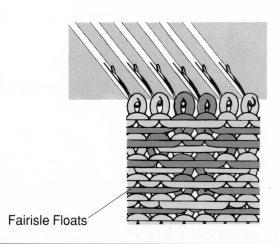

Fairisle Floats

The fairisle fabrics in this book have been designed so that long floats are limited. However, it is useful to know how to deal with designs that have long floats. After every row of knitting take the centre of each float and place it in the hook of the needle above. This will catch in the old stitch on the next row and make the back of the fabric tidy without affecting the front. Alternativly, floats can be gathered into groups and tied up with another thread after knitting.

Motifs

Motifs are fairisle patterns worked over a limited area. Consult your manual for details on how to set your machine to knit single motifs. As motifs only cover a small part of the work it is acceptable to have longer floats. See section on Floats for methods of dealing with them.

To avoid the contrast yarn or yarns of the motif separating from the background yarn, use the following technique. Prepare two 50 cm lengths of background yarn (one for either edge of the motif). On the side nearest the carriage put the end of one of the lengths of yarn into the hook of the first needle next to the edge of the motif. Repeat this after each row of knitting so that the two lengths of yarn bind the edges of the motif to the background fabric.

Intarsia

Intarsia is a technique for colour patterning where the yarn is laid in manually so it is suitable for most types of machine. Each colour knits back and forth within its own shape therefore there are no floats and no limit to the number of colours that can be used or the size of the motif or pattern. This technique is ideal for producing multi-coloured geometrics and picture knitting. As the method varies between machines consult your machine manual for more detailed instructions.

The intarsia charts are reversed because the work is done with the back of the fabric facing. You may find it helpful to transfer the charts onto larger graph paper or an automatic shaping guide if you have one before commencing work. If you are inexperienced try a simple geometric first remembering to cross the yarns where different colours meet as shown.

When the work has been removed from the machine, sew ends of yarn in neatly on the back of the fabric.

Swiss Darning

For more complicated designs with individual stitches in a different colour it is often quicker and easier to Swiss darn them after the knitting has been removed from the machine. (See Intarsia charts XIV.1, XIV.8 and XIV.9). This is also a good method for correcting mistakes.

Use a tapestry needle threaded with the appropriate yarn. Bring the needle out at the base of the stitch to be darned, take it up and around the top of the stitch (under the stitch above). Take the needle back through the base of the same stitch, then up through the base of the next stitch to be worked.

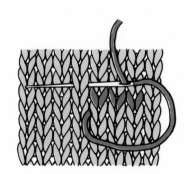

I.1

I.2

I.3

I.4

I. Wild Animals

Punchcard and electronic chart instructions and colour key on pages 9 to 11.

Chart A

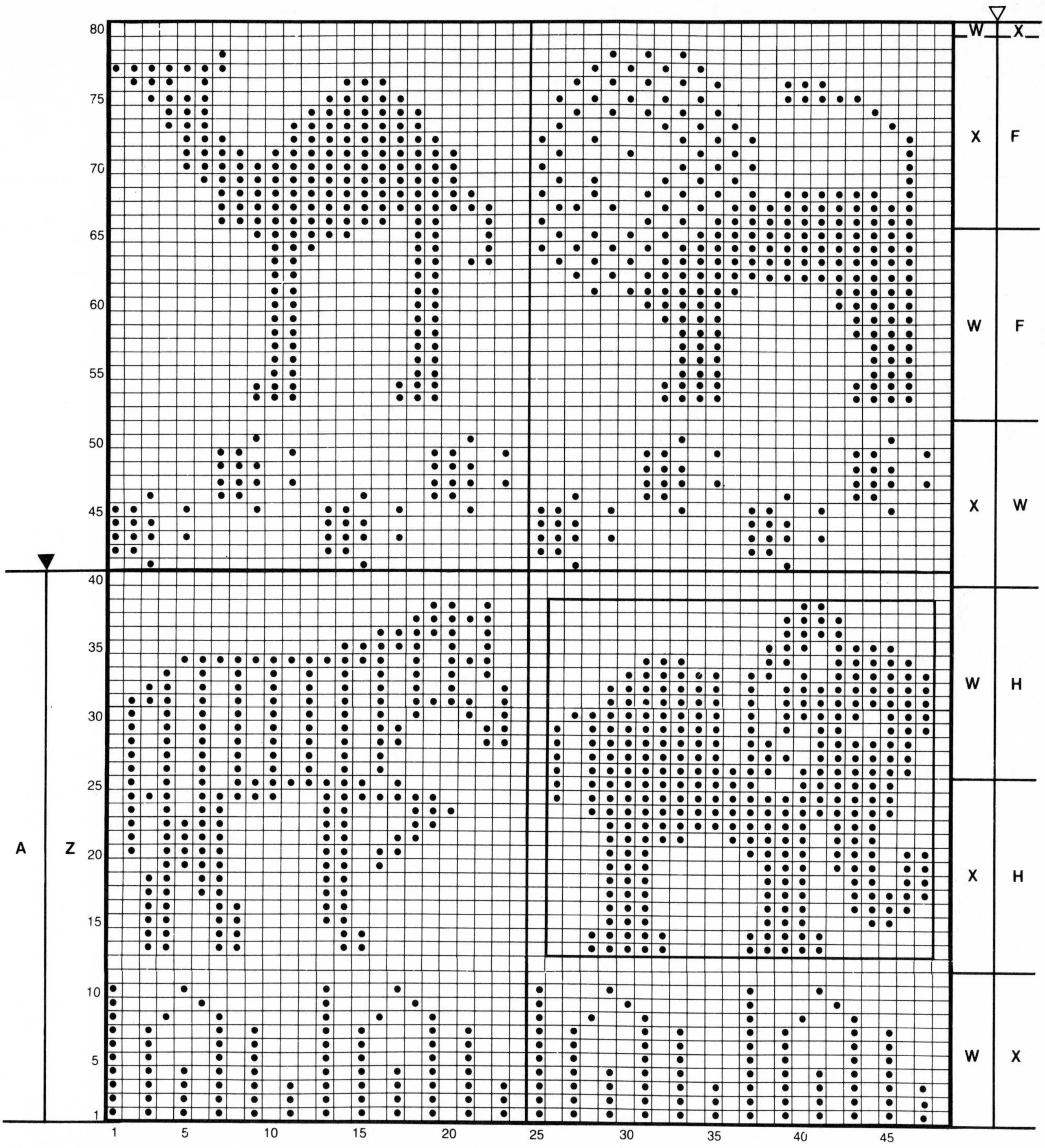

I.5 (Chart A) ▽

Electronic: Pattern Area (1,80,1,48)

Punchcard: Pattern Area (1,80,1,24) or (1,80,25,48). Colour Changes same as Electronic.

I.6 (Chart A)

Electronic: Motif Area (13,38,26,47)
Feeder 1 = E. Feeder 2 = F.
Double Width and Double Length.

I. Wild Animals

I.7 (Chart A)

Electronic: Pattern Area (41,80, 25,48).
Feeder 1 = Z. Feeder 2 = F.
Work 40 rows.
Move starting position 12 stitches and reverse.
Work 40 rows.
Repeat these 40 rows.

Punchcard: Pattern Area and Colour Changes same as Electronic.

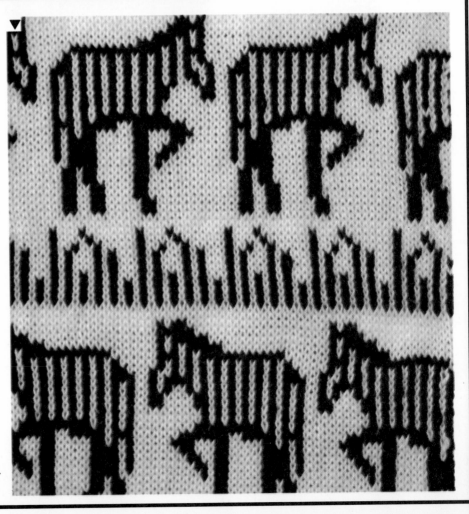

I.8 (Chart A) ▼

Electronic: Pattern Area (1,40,1,24).
Work 40 rows.
Move starting position 12 stitches and reverse.
Work 40 rows.
Repeat these 40 rows.

Punchcard: Pattern Area and Colour. Changes same as Electronic.

Punchcard and electronic chart instructions and colour key on pages 9 to 11.

I.9

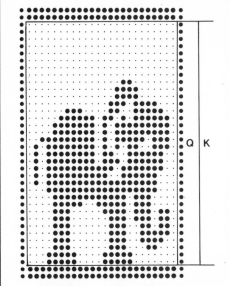

Q K

I.10

I.11

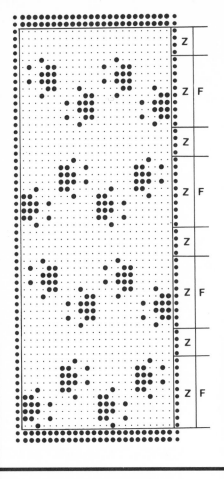

Z
Z F
Z
Z F
Z
Z F
Z
Z F

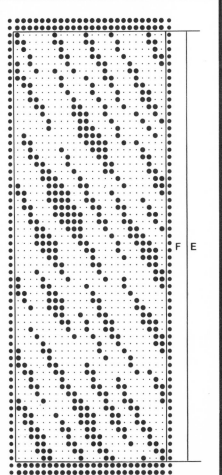

F E

I.12

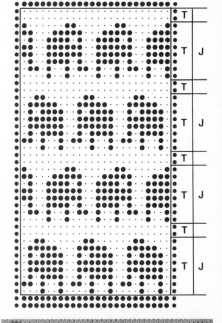

T
T J
T
T J
T
T J
T
T J

I. Wild Animals

I.13

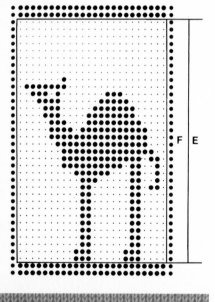

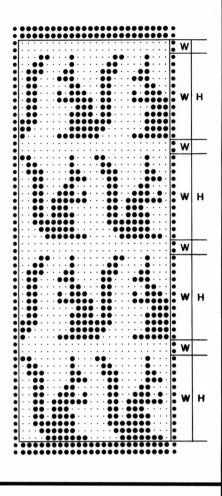

I.14

I.15

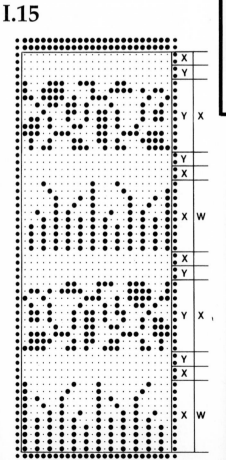

I.16

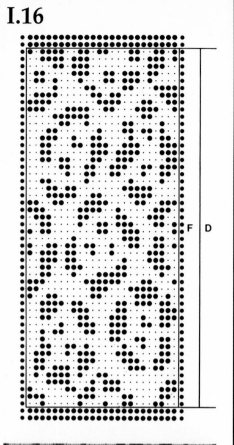

Punchcard and electronic chart instructions and colour key on pages 9 to 11.

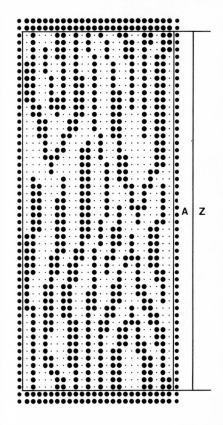

I.17

Electronic: Motif Area (1,78,1,60)
Feeder 1 = F. Feeder 2 = P.

I. Wild Animals

I.19

Electronic: Motif area (1,133,1,60)
Feeder 1 = E, Feeder 2 = F.

I.20

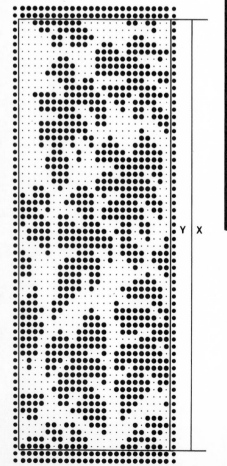

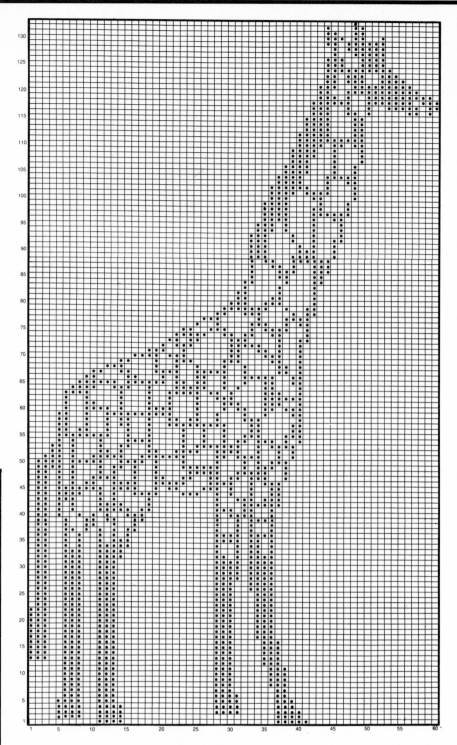

Punchcard and electronic chart instructions and colour key on pages 9 to 11.

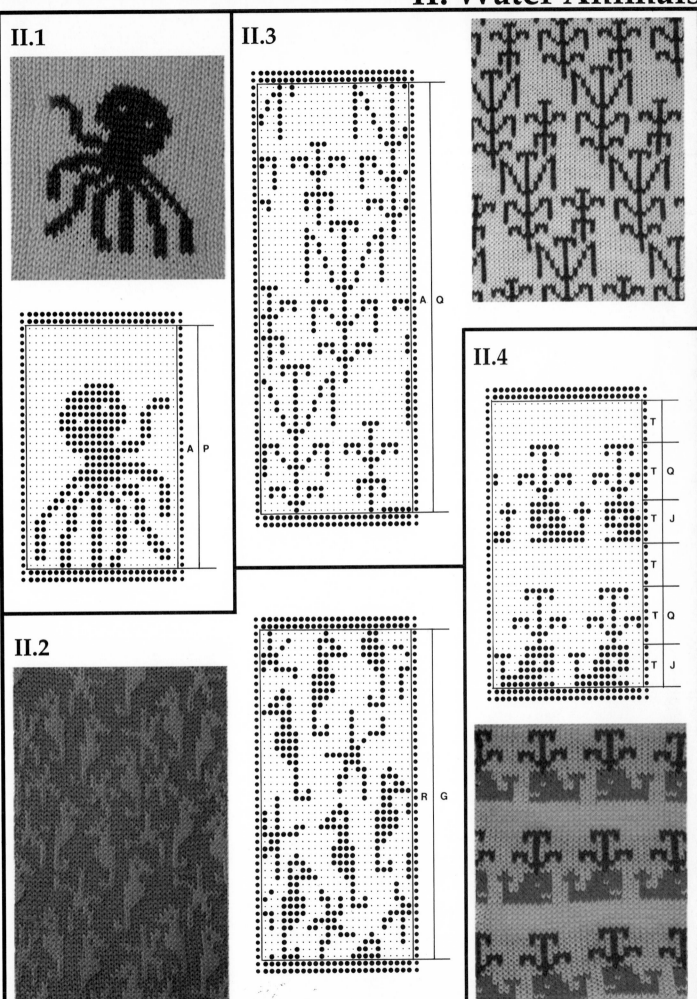

II.1

II.3

II.4

II.2

II. Water Animals

Punchcard and electronic chart instructions and colour key on pages 9 to 11.

Chart B

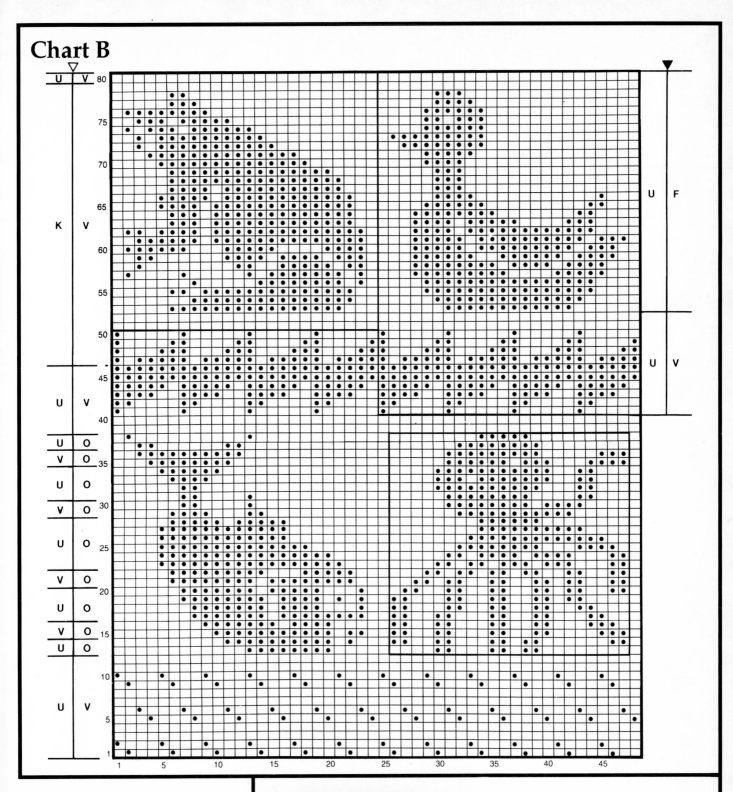

II.5 (Chart B) ▽

Electronic: Pattern Area (1,80,1,48)

Punchcard: Pattern Area (1,80,1,24) or (1,80,25,48). Colour Changes same as Electronic.

II.6 (Chart B)

Electronic: Motif Area (13, 38,26,47)
Feeder 1 = K. Feeder 2 = U.
Double Width and Double Length.

II. Water Animals

II.7 (Chart B) ▼

Electronic: Pattern Area (41,80, 25,48)
Work 40 rows.
Move starting position 12 stitches and reverse.
Work 40 rows.
Repeat these 40 rows.

Punchcard: Pattern Area and Colour changes same as Electronic.

II.8 (Chart B)

Electronic: Pattern Area (51,80,1,24)
Feeder 1 = O. Feeder 2 = P.
Work 40 rows.
Move starting position 12 stitches, reverse and work 40 rows in negative.
Repeat these 80 rows.

Punchcard: Pattern Area (51,80,1, 24)
Feeder 1 = O. Feeder 2 = P.
Work 40 rows.
Feeder 1 = P. Feeder 2 = O.
Work 40 rows.
Repeat these 80 rows.

Punchcard and electronic chart instructions and colour key on pages 9 to 11.

II.9

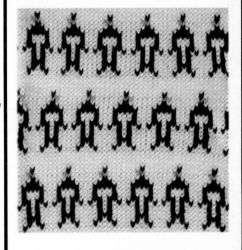

V G

II.12

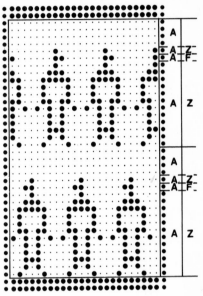

A

A Z
A F

A Z

A

A Z
A F

A Z

II.10

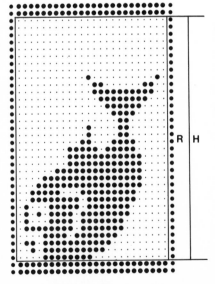

R H

II.11

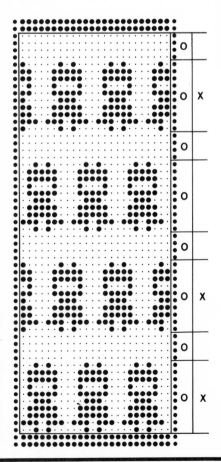

O

O X

O

O

O

O X

O

O X

25

II. Water Animals

II.13

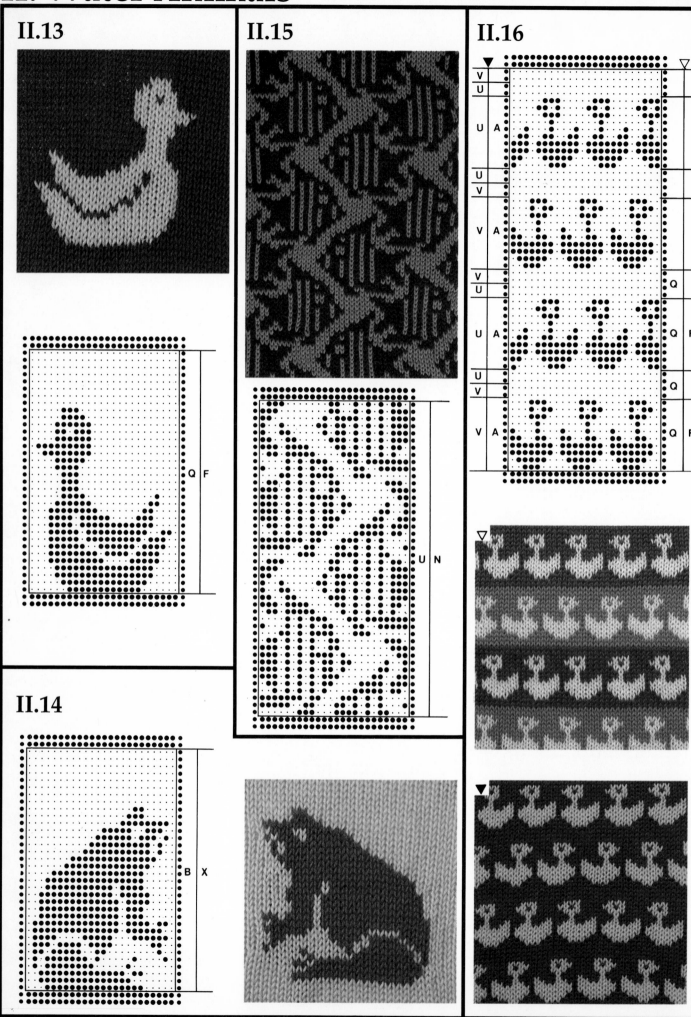

II.15

II.16

II.14

Punchcard and electronic chart instructions and colour key on pages 9 to 11.

III.1

Electronic: Motif Area (1,69,1,48)

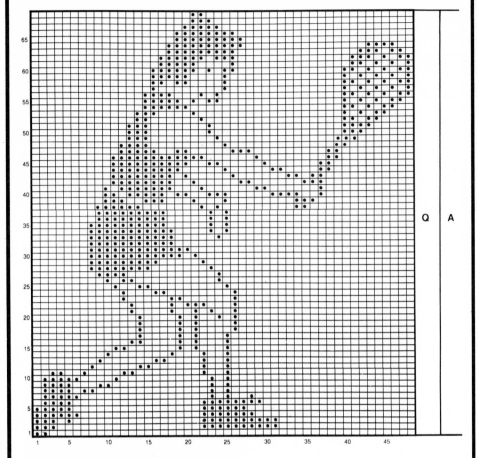

III.3

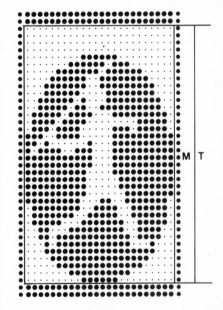

III.2

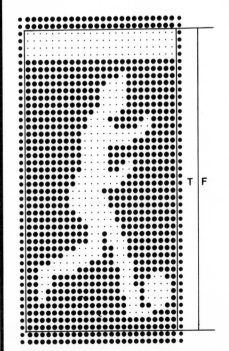

III. Sport

III.4

Electronic: Motif Area (1,74,1,48)

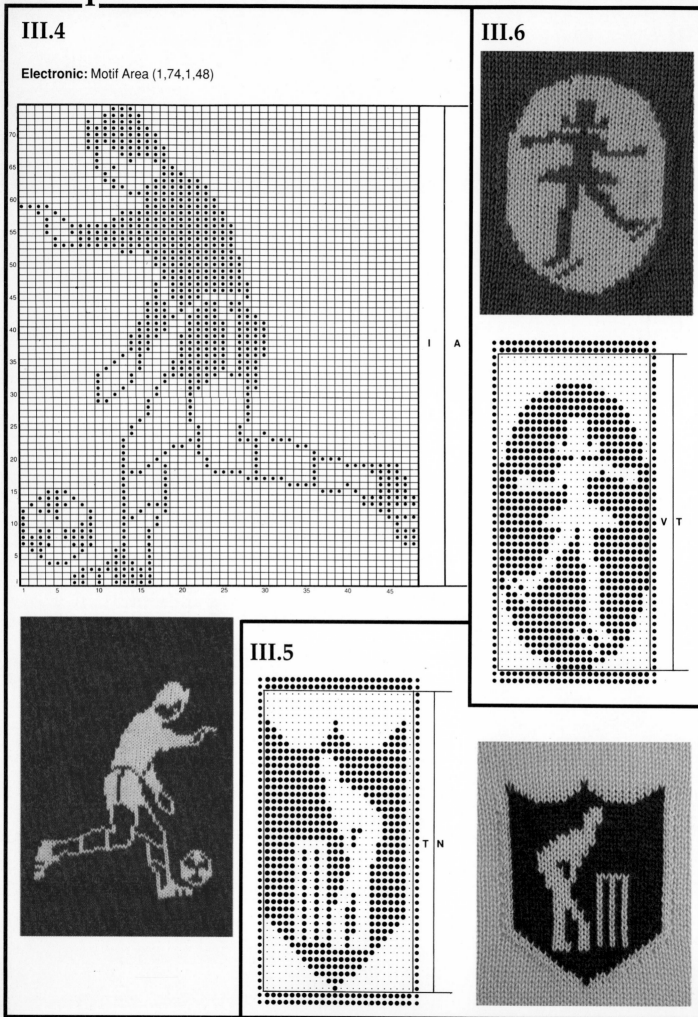

III.6

III.5

III.7

A I

III.8

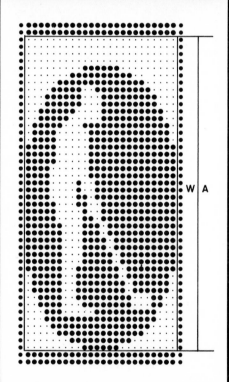

W A

III.9

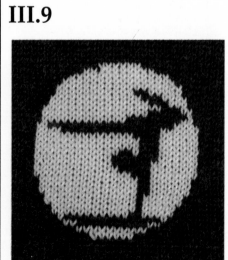

III.10

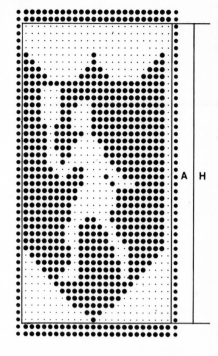

A H

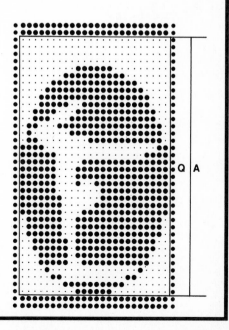

Q A

IV. Transport

Punchcard and electronic chart instructions and colour key on pages 9 to 11.

Chart C

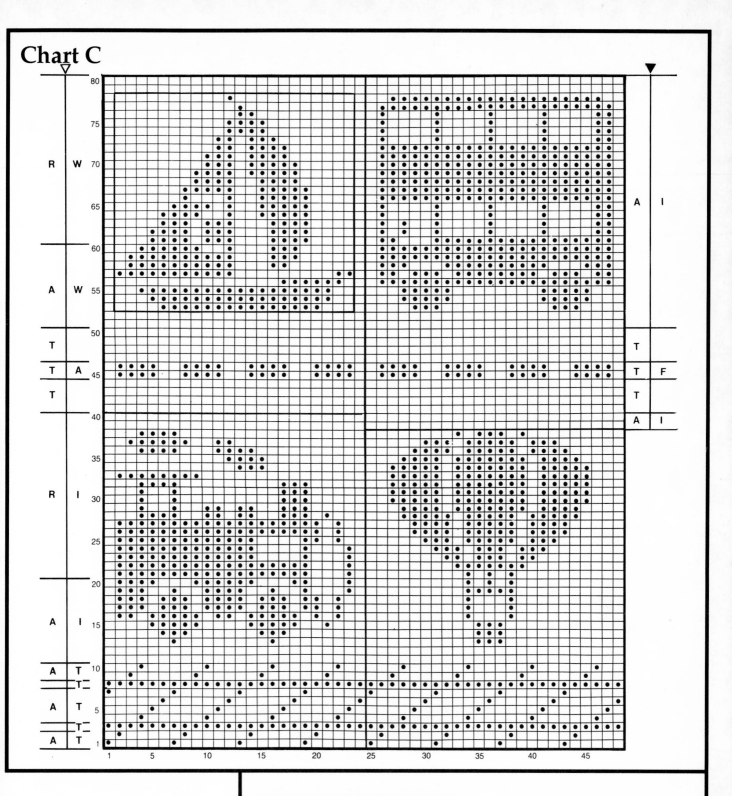

IV.1 (Chart C) ▽

Electronic: Pattern Area (1,80,1,48)

Punchcard: Pattern Area (1,80,1,24) or (1,80,25,48). Colour Changes same as Electronic

IV.2 (Chart C)

Electronic: Motif Area (53,78,2,23) Feeder 1 = F. Feeder 2 = T. Double Width and Double Length.

IV. Transport

IV.3 (Chart C) ▼

Electronic: Pattern Area (39,80, 25,48)
Work 42 rows.
Move starting position 12 stitches and reverse.
Work 42 rows.
Repeat these 84 rows.

Punchcard: Pattern Area and Colour Changes same as electronic.

IV.4 (Chart C)

Electronic: Pattern Area (1,42,1,24)
Feeder 1 = A. Feeder 2 = R.
Work 10 rows.
Feeder 1 = I. Feeder 2 = W.
Work 32 rows.
Move starting position and reverse.
Feeder 1 = A. Feeder 2 = R.
Work 10 rows
Feeder 1 = I. Feeder 2 = W.
Work 32 rows.
Repeat these 84 rows.

Punchcard: Pattern Area and Colour Change same as electronic.

Punchcard and electronic chart instructions and colour key on pages 9 to 11.

IV.5

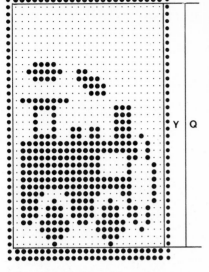

IV.7

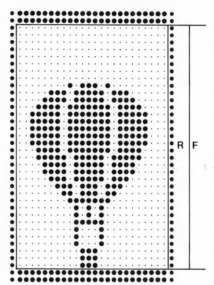

IV.8

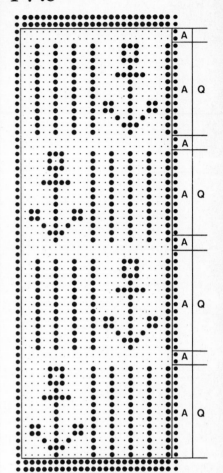

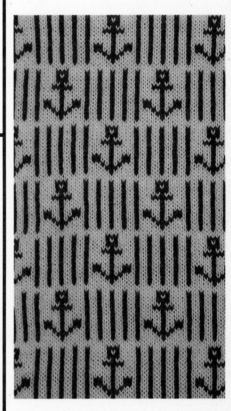

IV.6

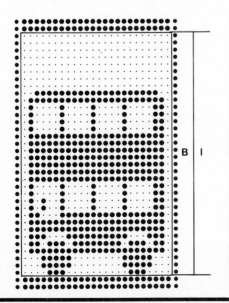

33

V. Astrology

V.1

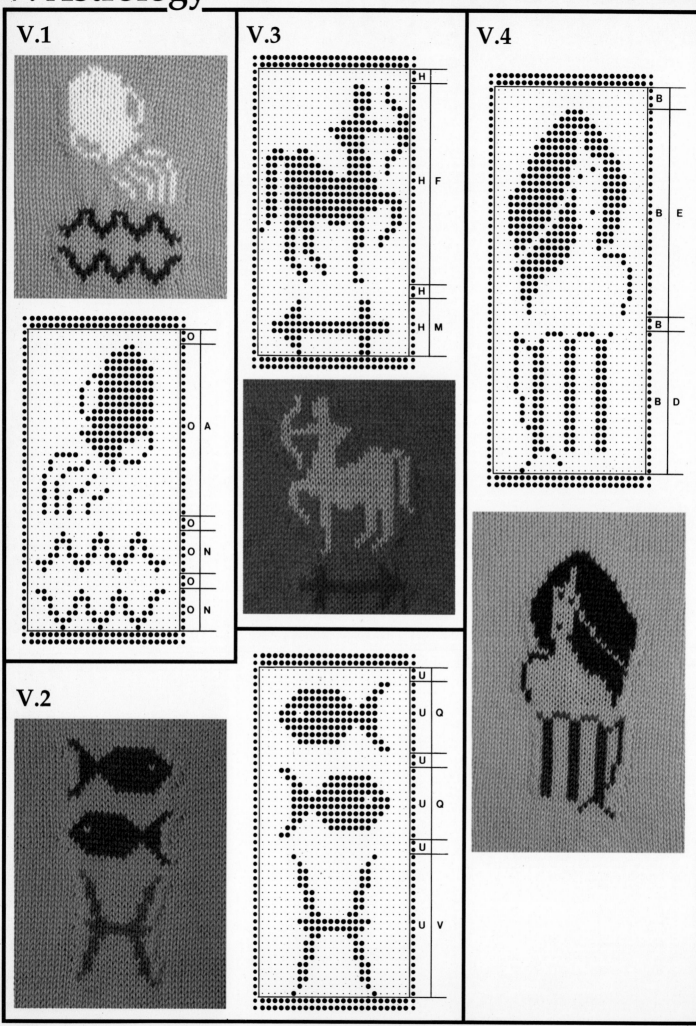

V.2

V.3

V.4

Punchcard and electronic chart instructions and colour key on pages 9 to 11.

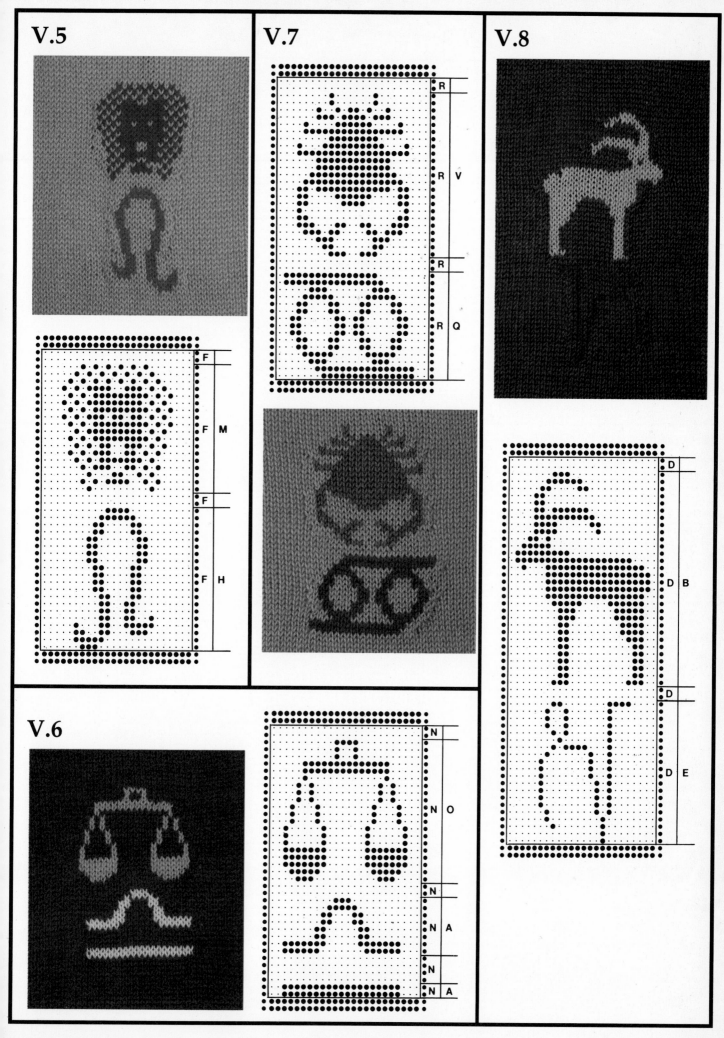

V.9 Electronic: Pattern Area (1,146,1,60)

N F

Punchcard and electronic chart instructions and colour key on pages 9 to 11.

V. Astrology

V.10

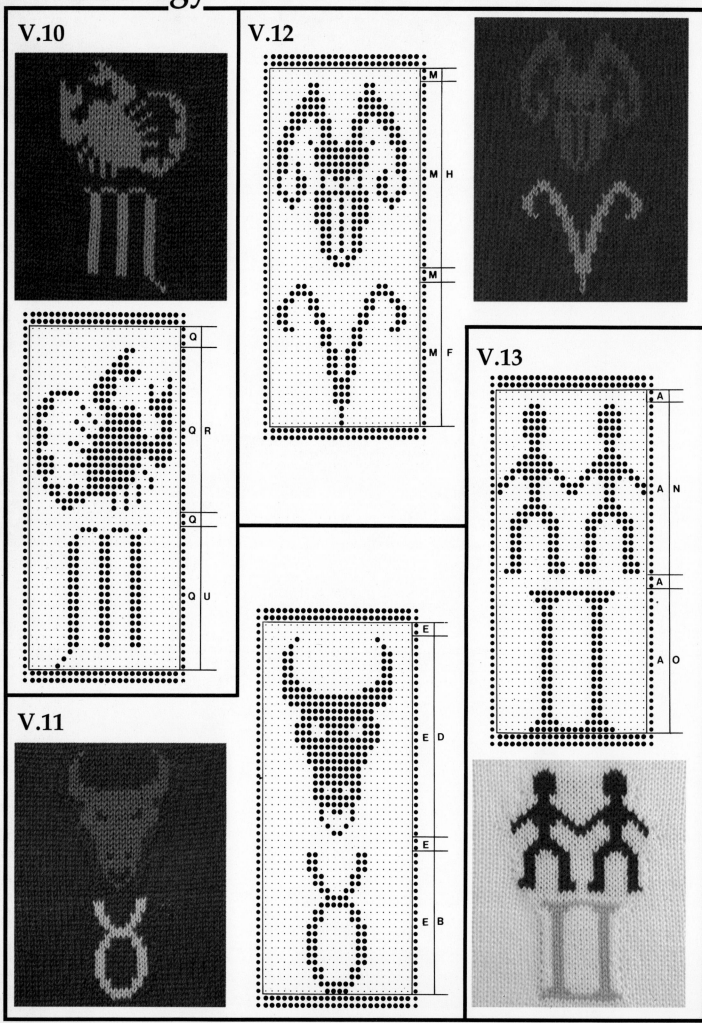

V.12

V.11

V.13

Punchcard and electronic chart instructions and colour key on pages 9 to 11.

VI. 1

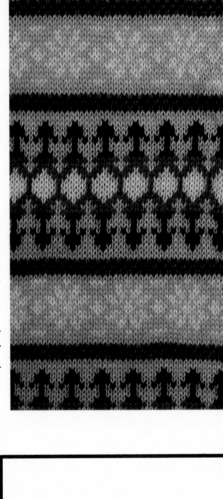

VI.2

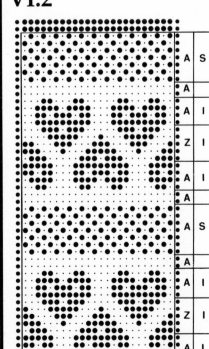

VI.3

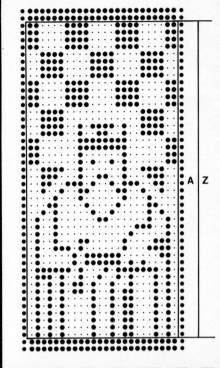

VI. Festive

VI.4

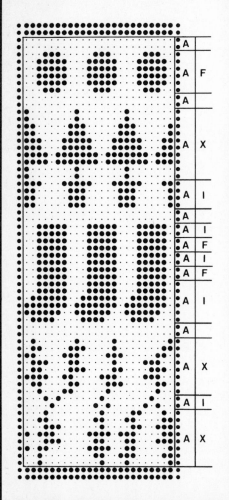

VI.5

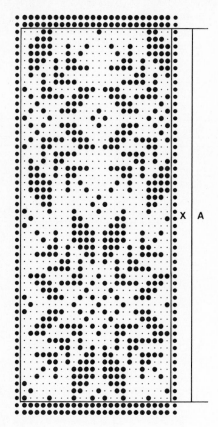

VI.6

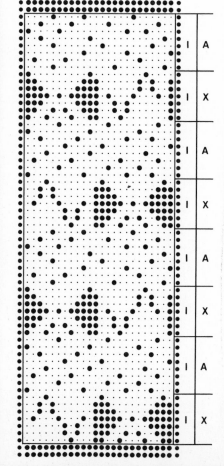

Punchcard and electronic chart instructions and colour key on pages 9 to 11.

VI.7

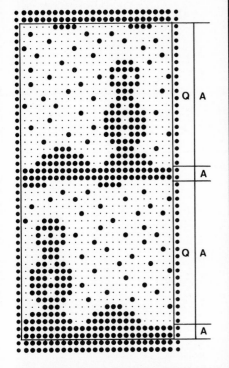

VI.8 Electronic: Pattern Area (1,42,1,30)

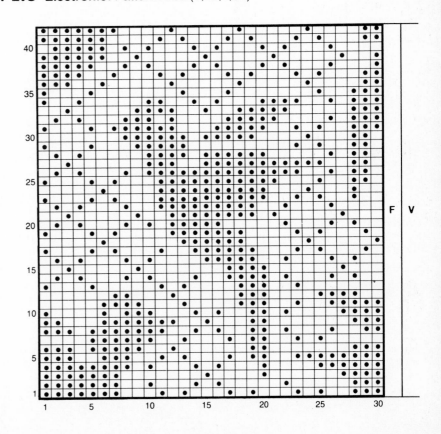

41

VI. Festive

VI.9 Electronic: Pattern Area (1,55,1,50)

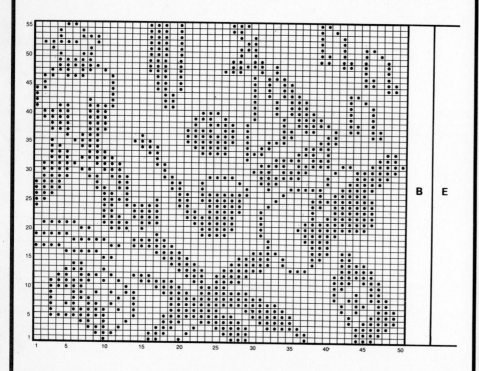

VI.10

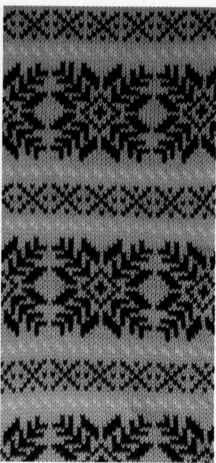

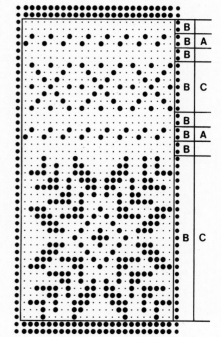

Punchcard and electronic chart instructions and colour key on pages 9 to 11.

VI.11

VI.12

VI.13

43

VI. Festive

VI.14 **Electronic:** Pattern Area (1,72,1,32)

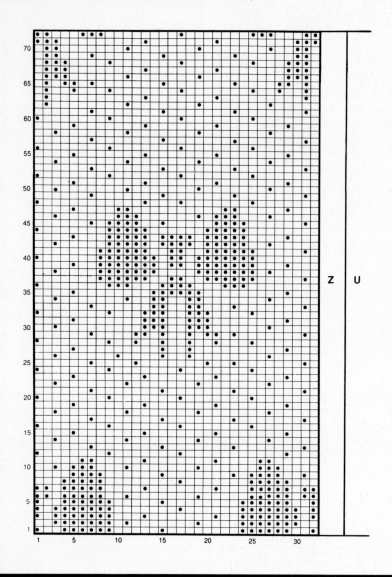

Z   U

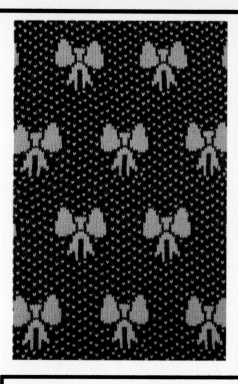

VI.16

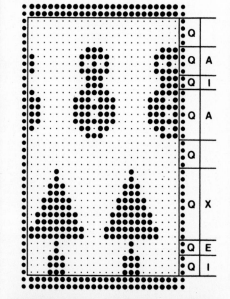

Q		
Q	A	
Q	I	
Q	A	
Q		
Q	X	
Q	E	
Q	I	

VI.15

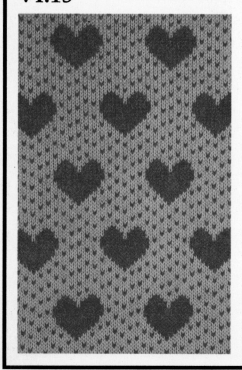

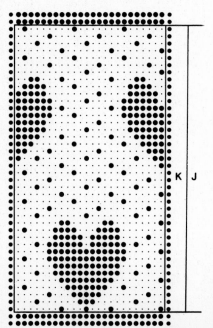

K J

Punchcard and electronic chart instructions and colour key on pages 9 to 11.

VI.17

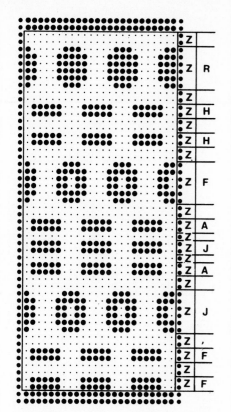

Z		
Z	R	
Z		
Z	H	
Z		
Z	H	
Z		
Z	F	
Z		
Z	A	
Z	J	
Z	A	
Z		
Z	J	
Z	,	
Z	F	
Z	F	

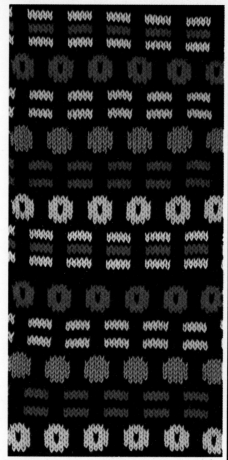

VI.19

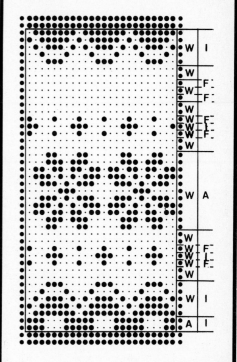

W	I	
W		
W	F	
W		
W	F	
W	I	
W	F	
W		
W		
W	A	
W		
W	F	
W	F	
W		
W	I	
A	I	

VI.18

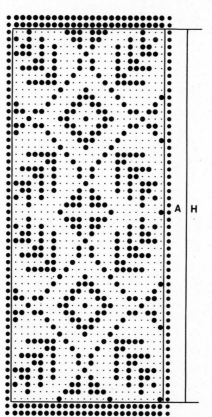

A H

VI. Festive

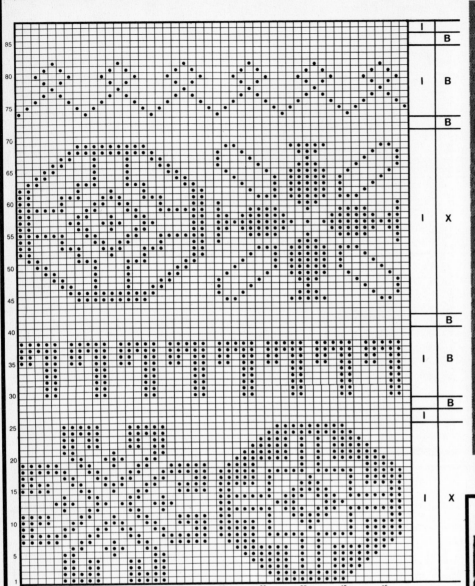

VI.20

Electronic: Pattern Area (1,88,1,48)

Punchcard: Pattern Area (1,88,1,24) or (1,88,25,48). Colour Change same as Electronic.

VI.21

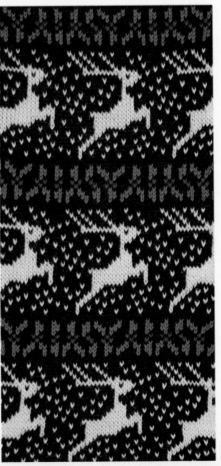

Punchcard and electronic chart instructions and colour key on pages 9 to 11.

VII.1

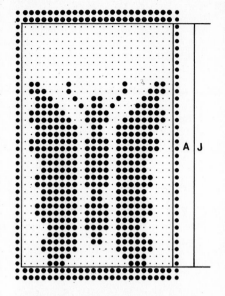

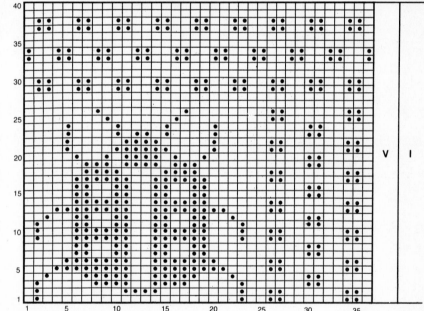

VII.2

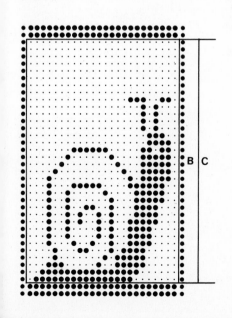

VII.3

Electronic: Pattern Area (1,40,1,36)

Punchcard: Pattern Area (1,40,1,24). Colour Changes same as Electronic.

VII. Creepy Crawlies

 Punchcard and electronic chart instructions and colour key on pages 9 to 11.

Chart D

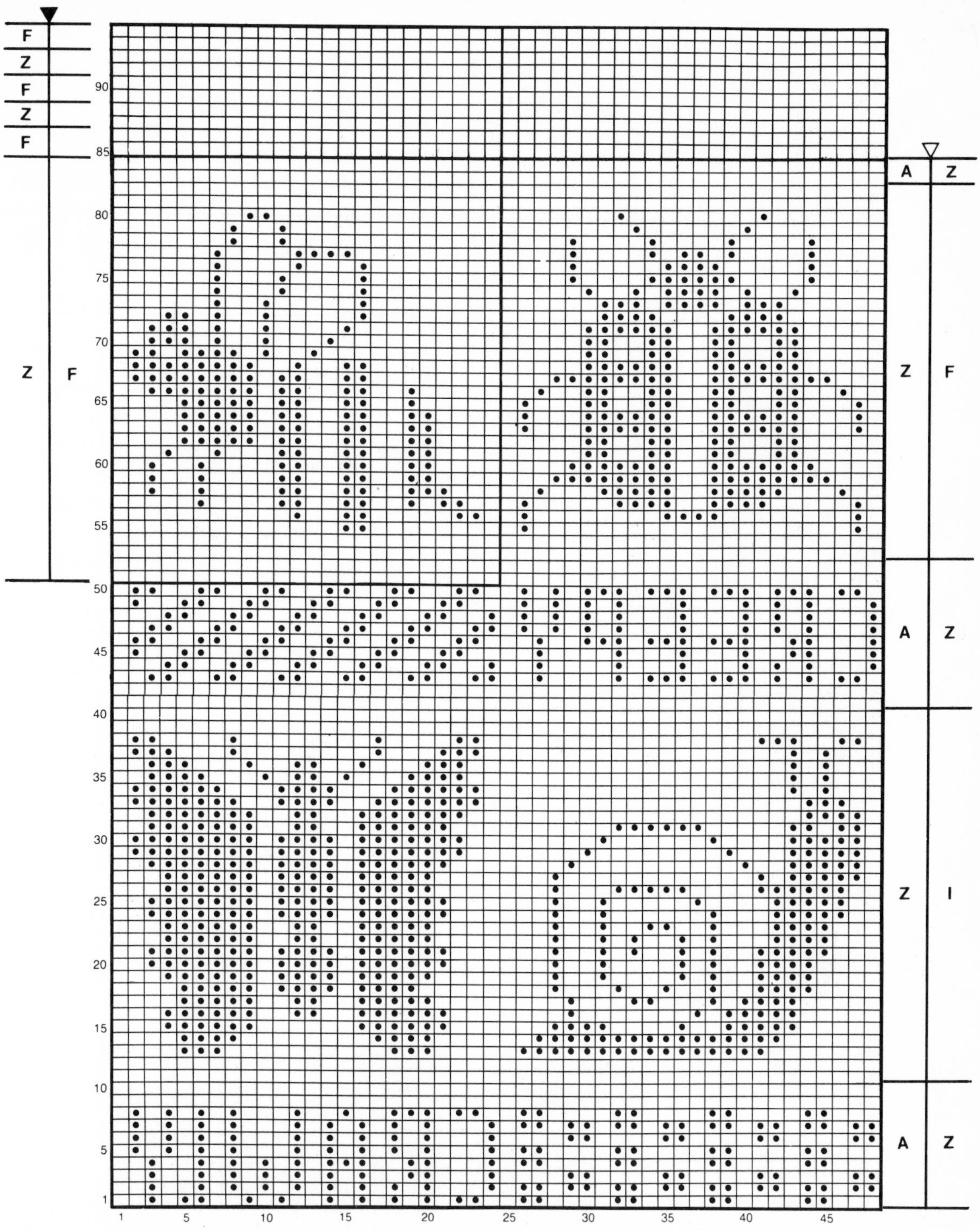
F
Z
F
Z
F
Z F
A Z
Z F
A Z
Z I
A Z

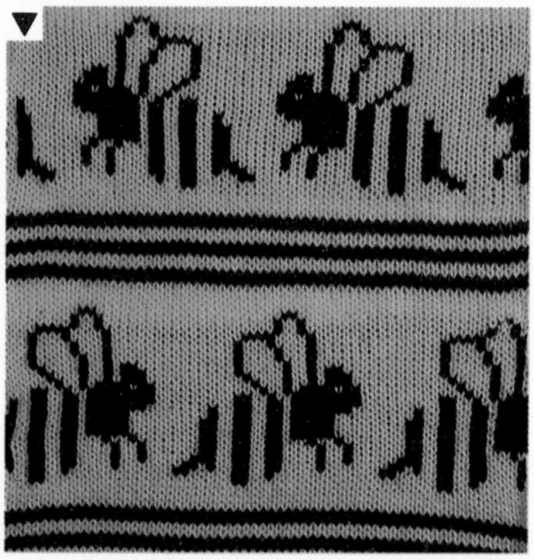

VII.4 (Chart D) ▽

Electronic: Pattern Area (1,84,1,48)

Punchcard: Pattern Area (1,84,1,24) or (1,84,25,48). Colour Changes same as Electronic.

VII.5 (Chart D) ▼

Electronic: Pattern Area (51,94,1,24)
Work 40 rows.
Move starting position 12 stitches and reverse.
Work 40 rows.
Repeat these 80 rows.

Punchcard: Pattern Area and Colour Changes same as Electronic.

VIII. Flora

VIII.1

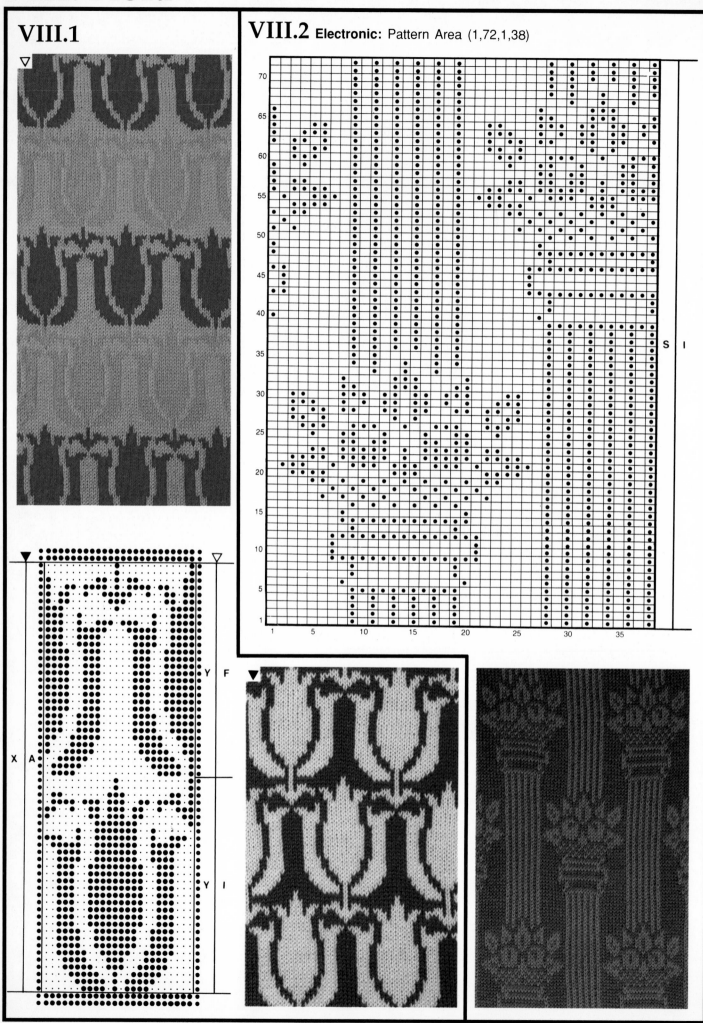

VIII.2 Electronic: Pattern Area (1,72,1,38)

Punchcard and electronic chart instructions and colour key on pages 9 to 11.

VIII.3 Electronic: Pattern Area (1,42,1,42)

VIII.4

VIII. Flora

VIII.5

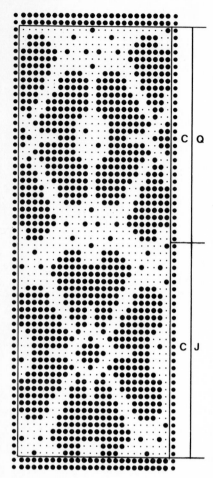

C | Q

C | J

VIII.6 Electronic: Pattern Area (1,70,1,45)

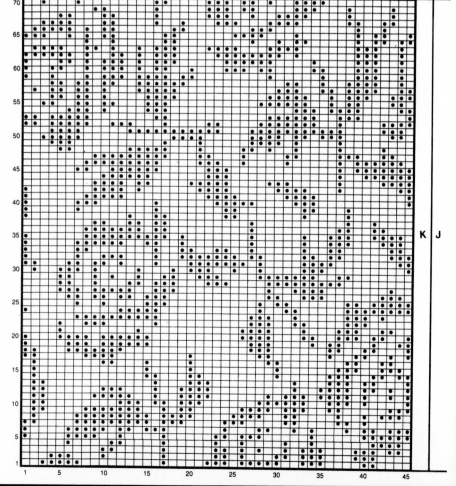

K | J

Punchcard and electronic chart instructions and colour key on pages 9 to 11.

VIII.7 Electronic: Pattern Area (1,42,1,42)

G V

VIII.8 Electronic: Pattern Area (1,73,1,33)

Y W

VIII. Flora

VIII.9

VIII.10

VIII.11

Punchcard and electronic chart instructions and colour key on pages 9 to 11.

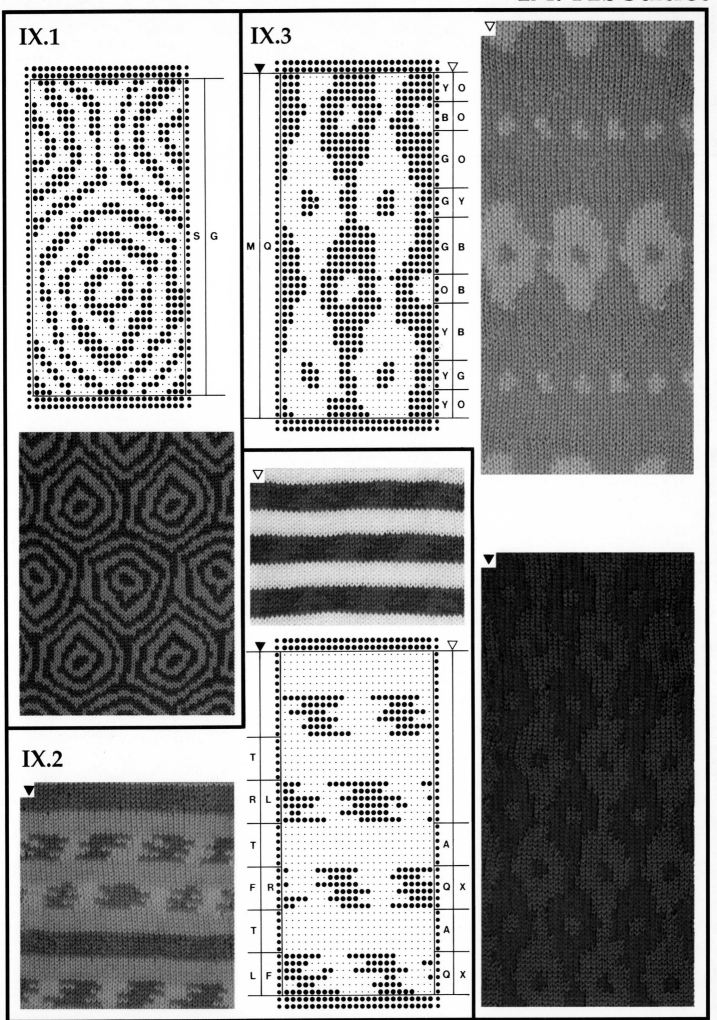

IX.1

IX.3

IX.2

IX. Abstract

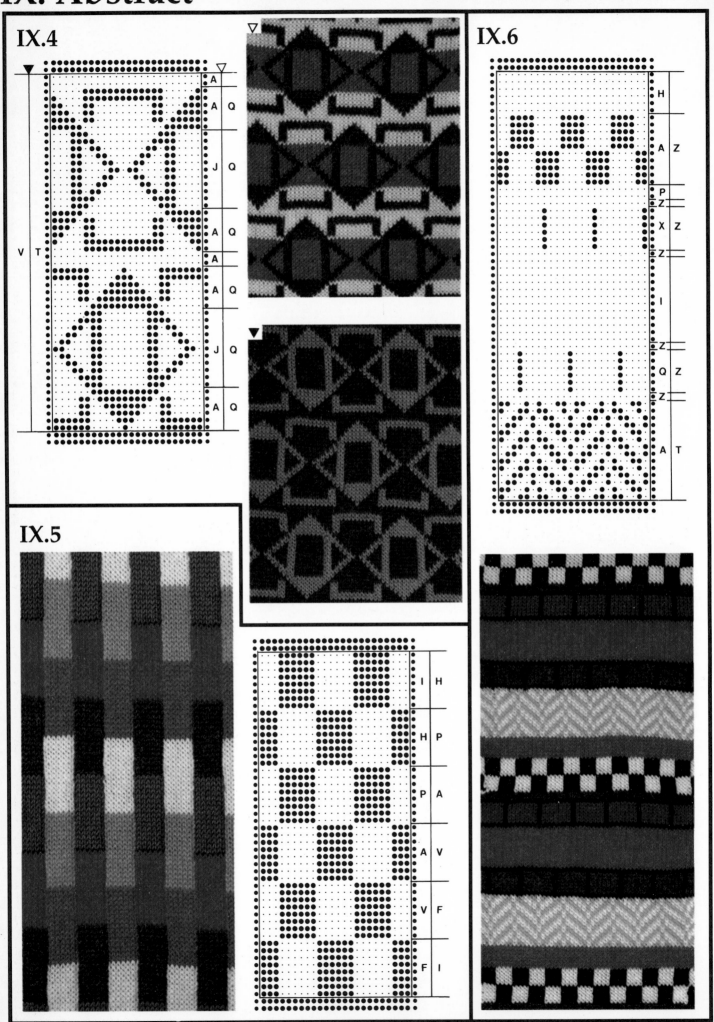

IX.4

IX.5

IX.6

Punchcard and electronic chart instructions and colour key on pages 9 to 11.

IX.7

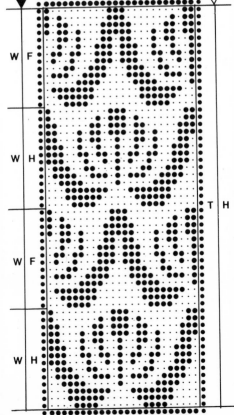

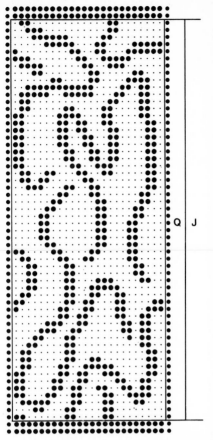

Q J

IX.9

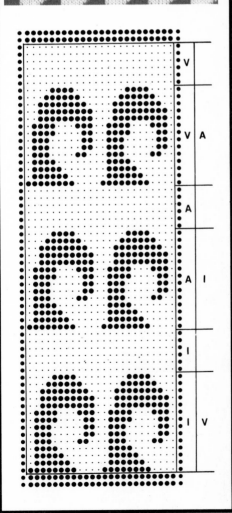

V
V A
A
A I
I
I V

IX.8

W F

W H

W F

W H

T H

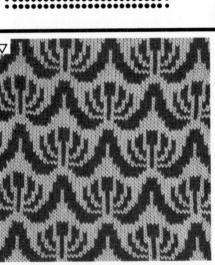

IX. Abstract

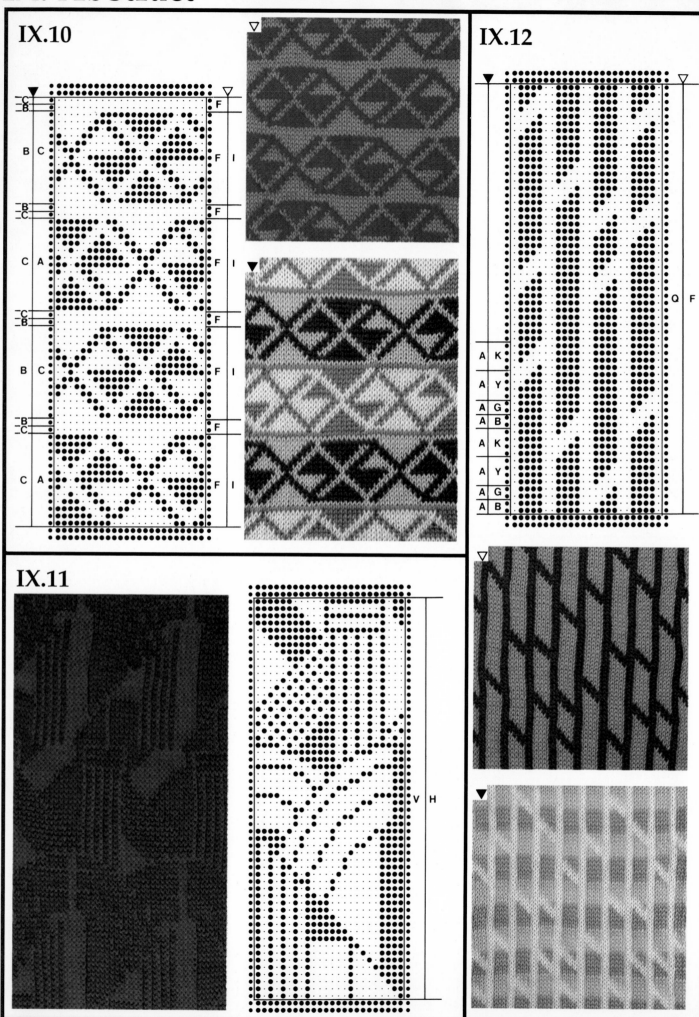

IX.10

IX.11

IX.12

Punchcard and electronic chart instructions and colour key on pages 9 to 11.

IX.13

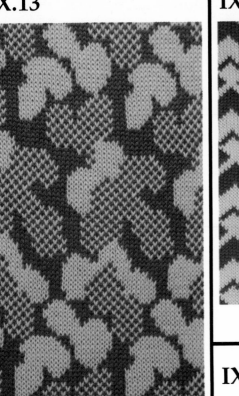

IX.14

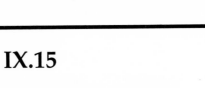

IX.15

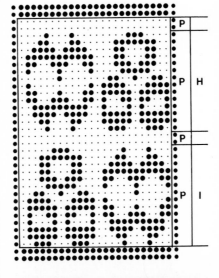

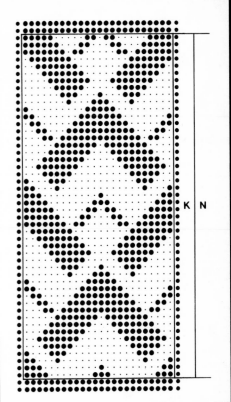

K N

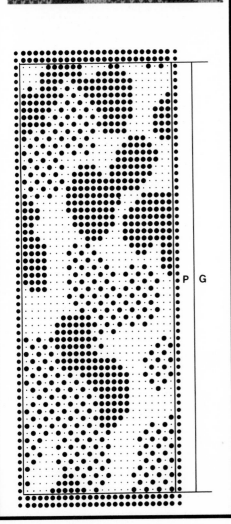

P G

P
P H
P
P I

IX.16

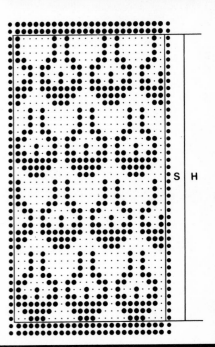

S H

X. Diamonds

X.1

A S

X.2

L Q
L M
Q F
A M
A Q

X.3

A W
W M
A M

X.4

X.6

X.7

X.5

XI. Ethnic

XI.1

Electronic: Pattern Area (1,102,1,30). Feeder 1 = Q. Feeder 2 = I

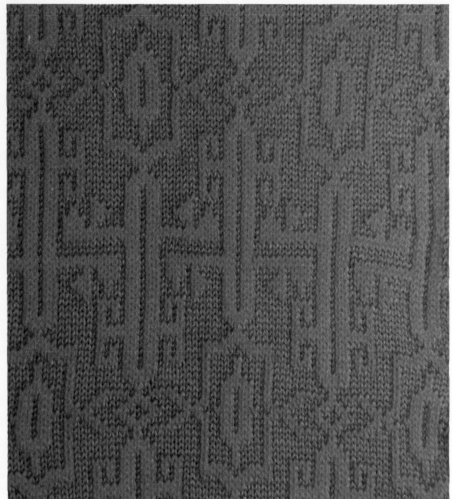

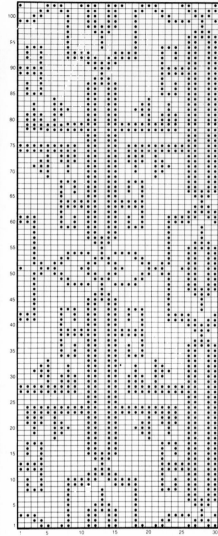

XI.2

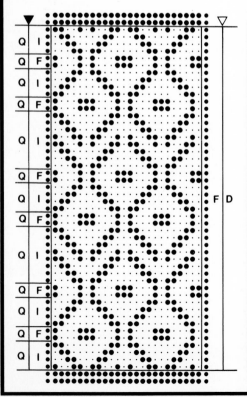

Punchcard and electronic chart instructions and colour key on pages 9 to 11.

XI.3

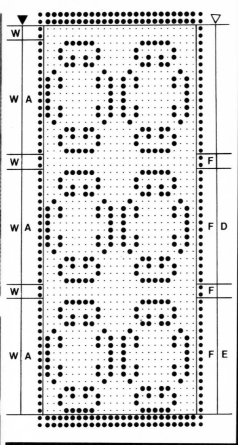

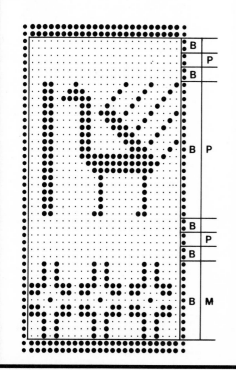

XI.4

XI.5

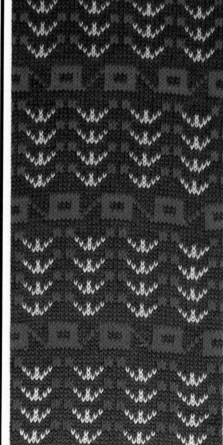

XI. Ethnic

XI.6

XI.7

XI.8

XI.9

XI.10

Electronic: Pattern Area (1,68,1,36)

XI.11

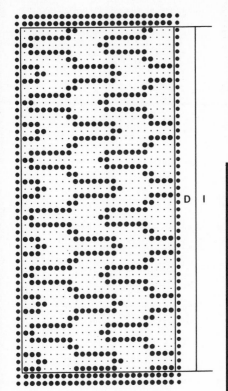

D I

XI.12

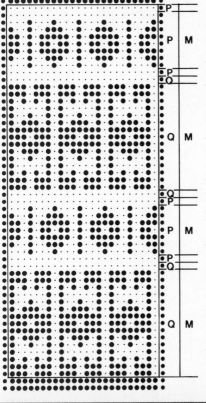

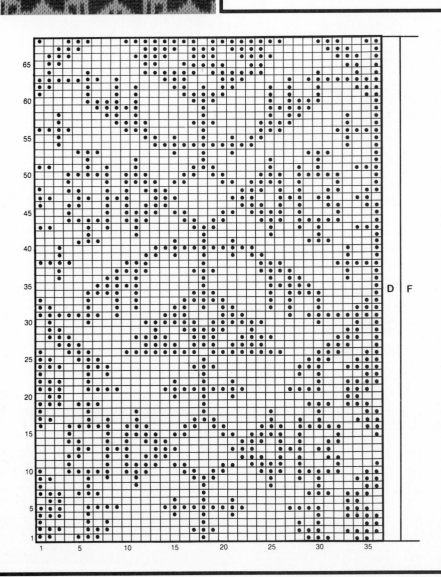

D F

XI. Ethnic

XI.13

XI.15

XI.16

XI.14

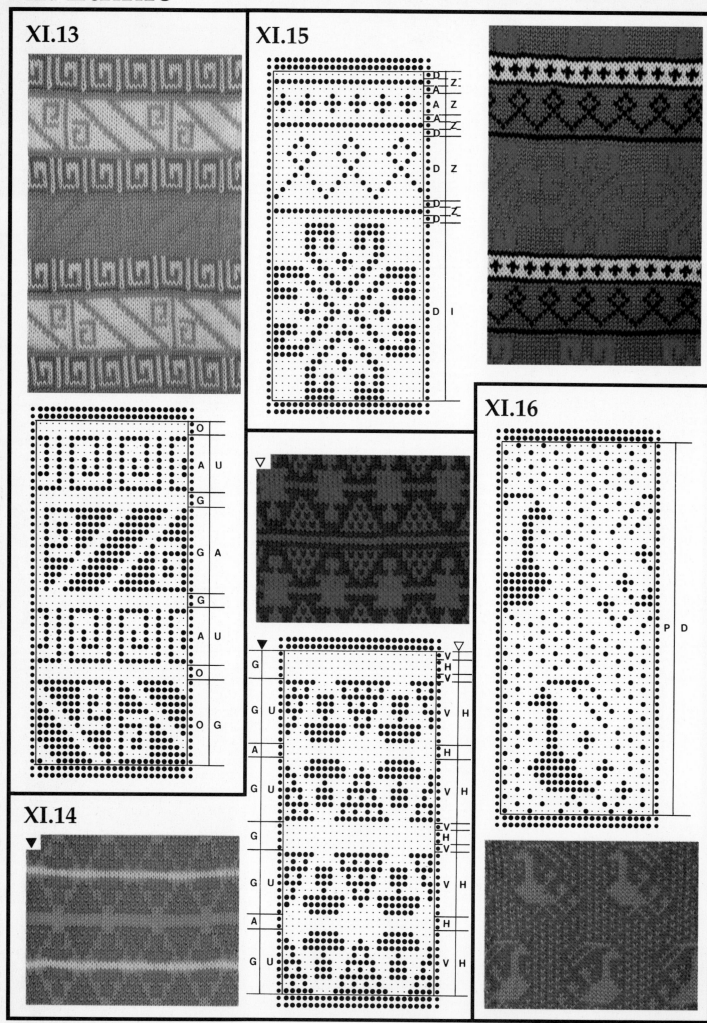

Punchcard and electronic chart instructions and colour key on pages 9 to 11.

XII.1

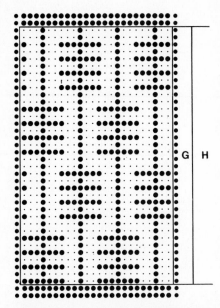

G H

XII.2

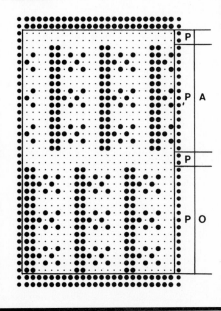

P
P
A
P
P O

XII.3

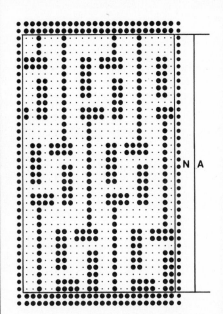

N A

XII.4

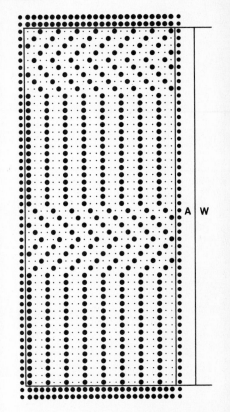

A W

XII. Optic

XII.5 **Electronic:** Pattern Area (1,32,1,42)

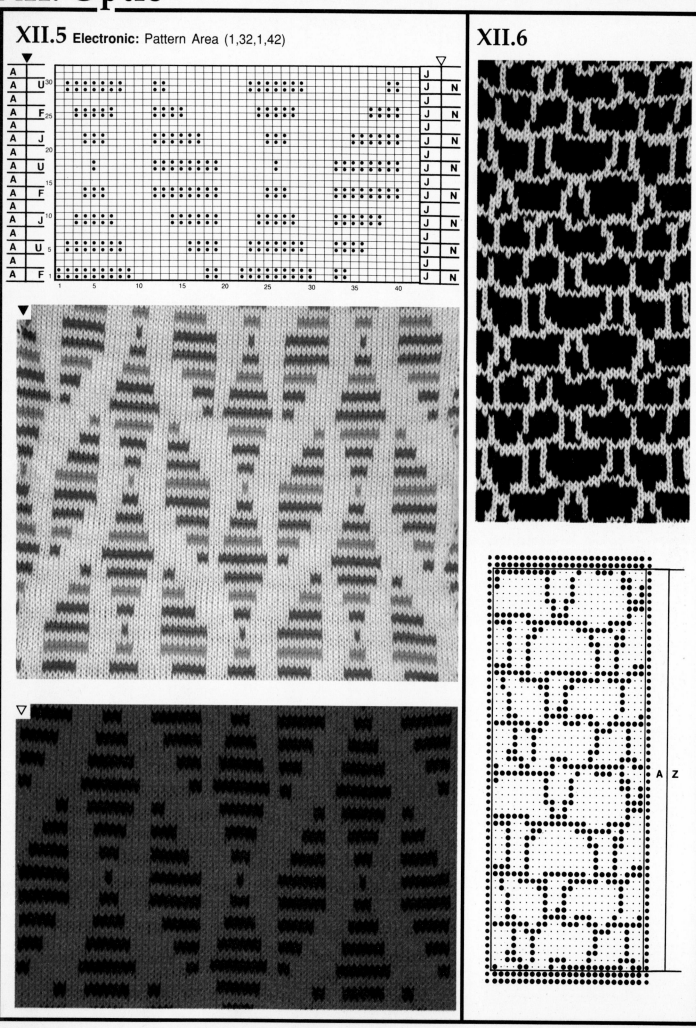

XII.6

Punchcard and electronic chart instructions and colour key on pages 9 to 11.

XII.7

Electronic: Pattern Area (1,52,1,40)

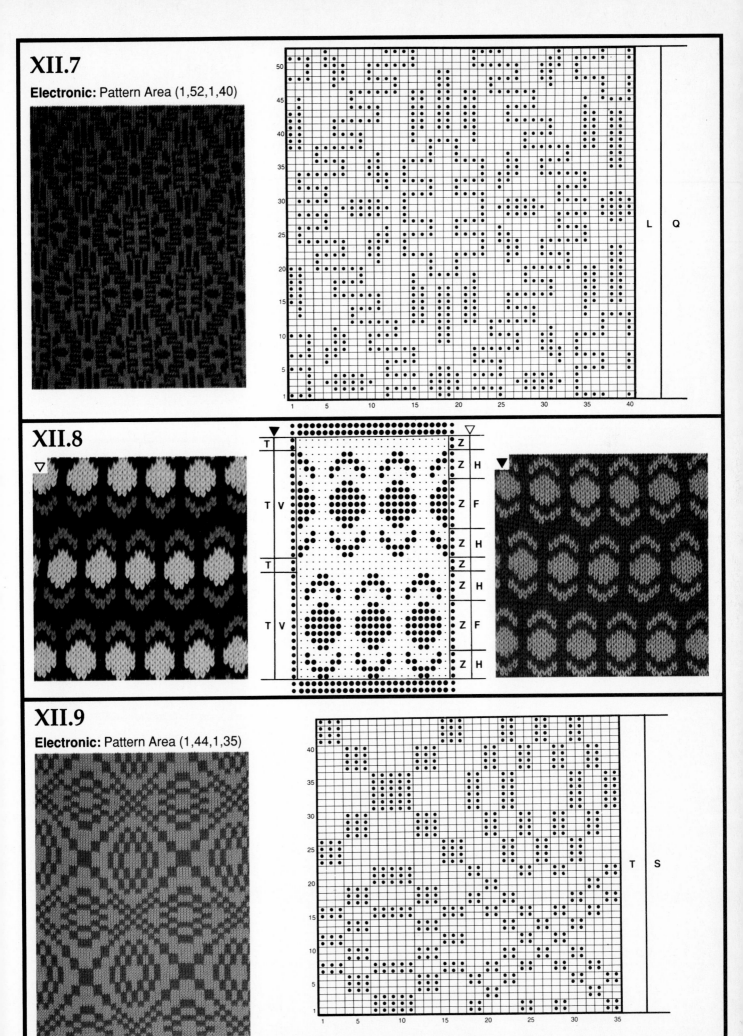

XII.8

XII.9

Electronic: Pattern Area (1,44,1,35)

XIII. Texture

XIII.1

XIII.2

XIII.3

XIII.4

Punchcard and electronic chart instructions and colour key on pages 9 to 11.

XIII.5

XIII.6

XIII.7

A	Q
A	I
A	Q
A	Q
A	Q
A	I
A	Q
A	Q

XIII.8

XIII. Texture

XIII.9

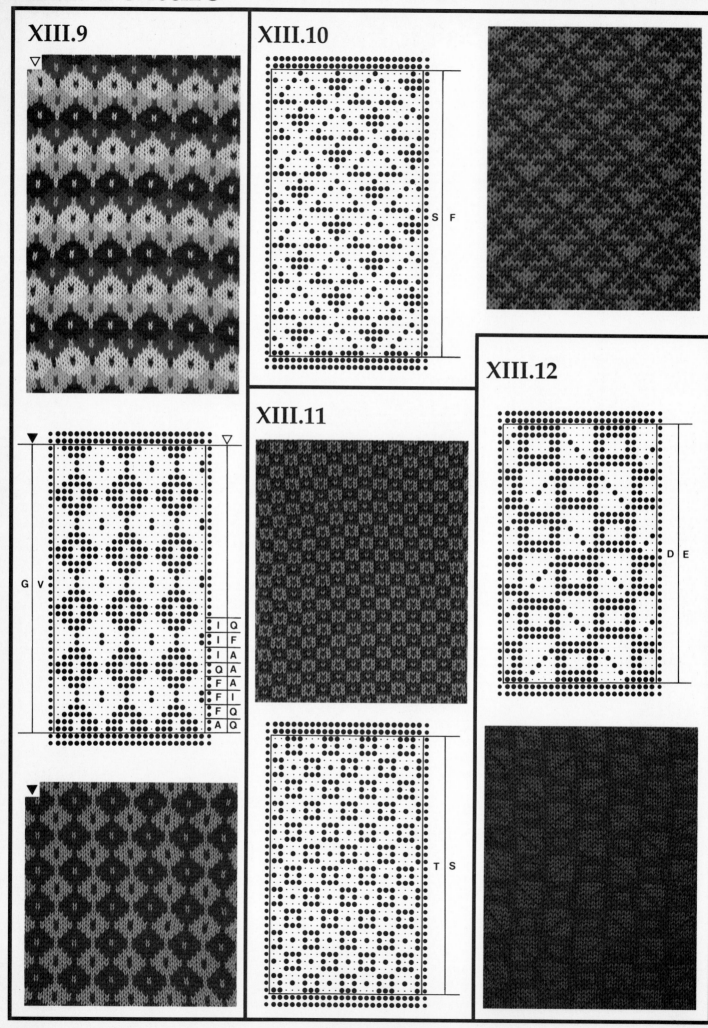

XIII.10

XIII.11

XIII.12

XIV.1

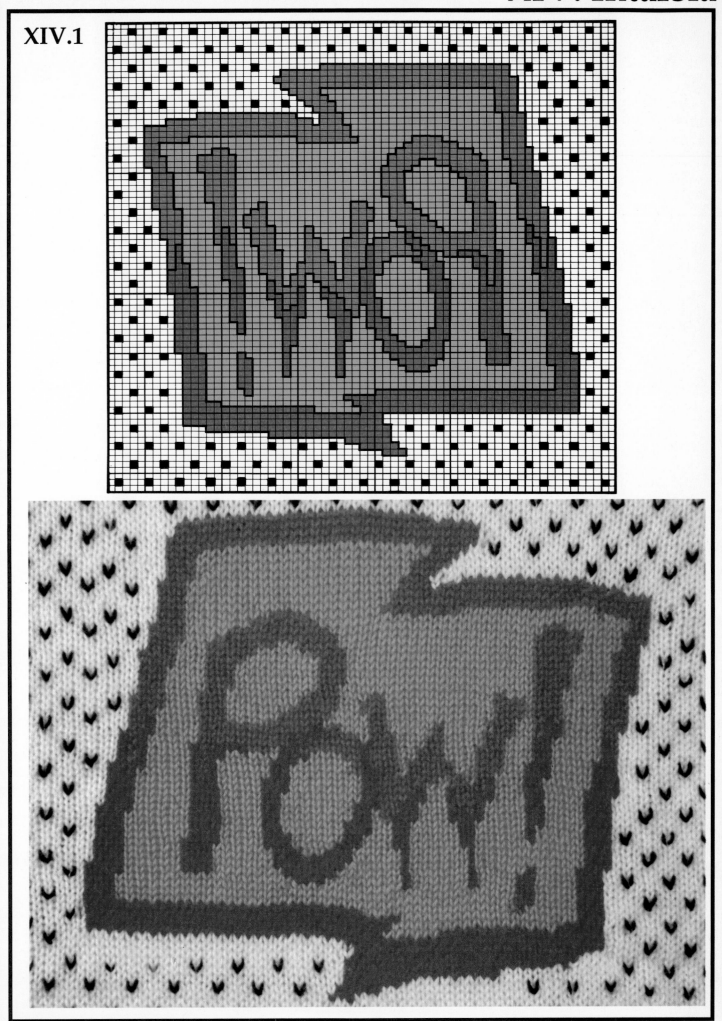

XIV. Intarsia

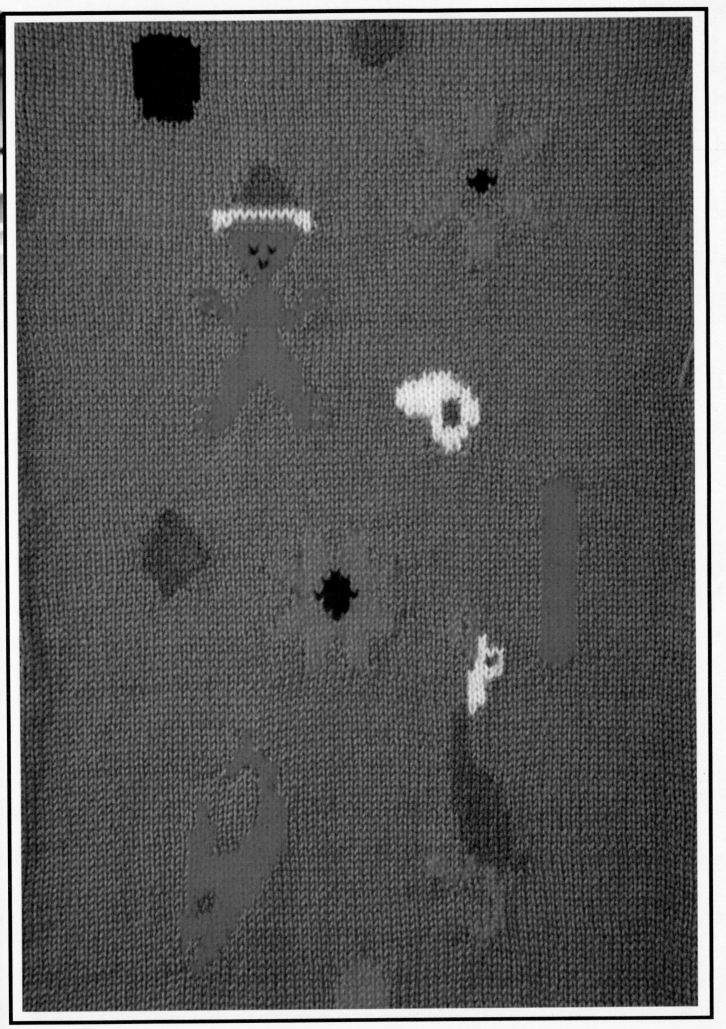

XIV. Intarsia

XIV.3

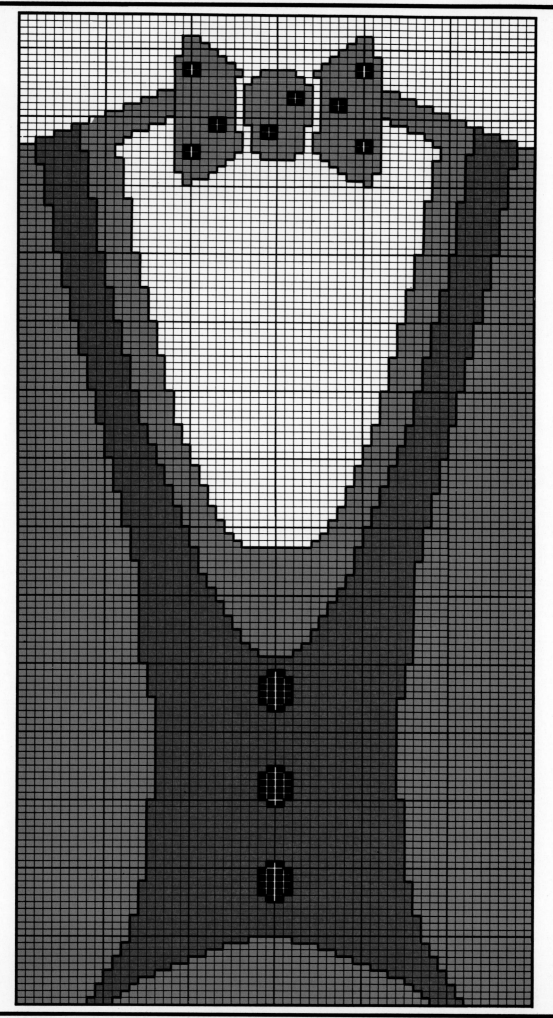

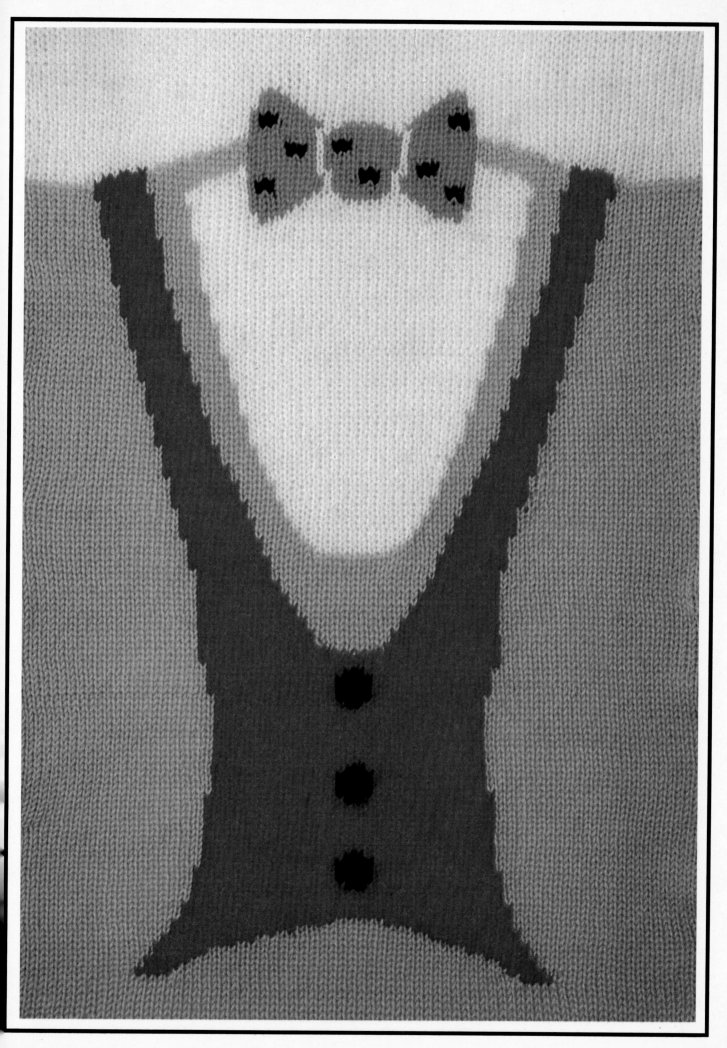

XIV. Intarsia

XIV.4

XIV. Intarsia

XIV.5

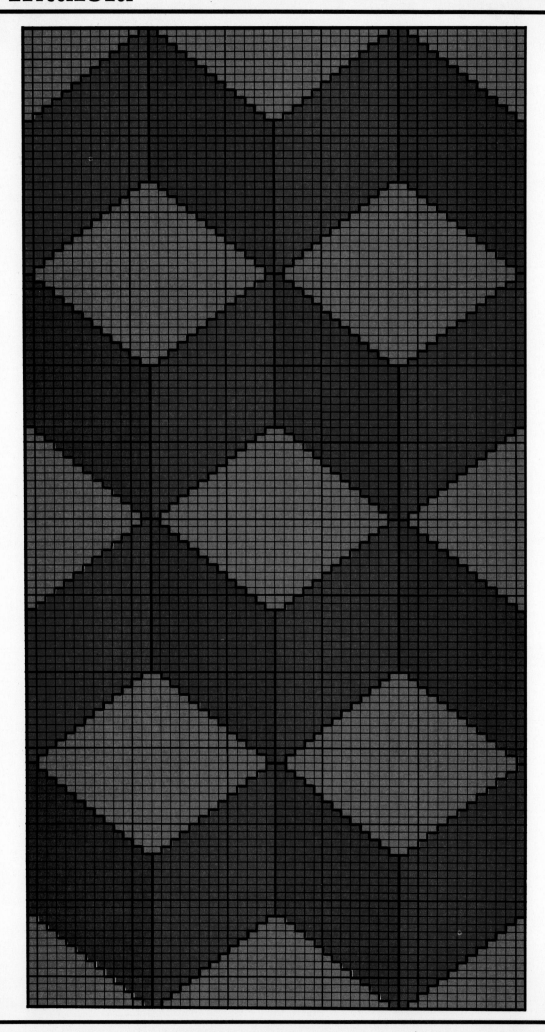

XIV. Intarsia

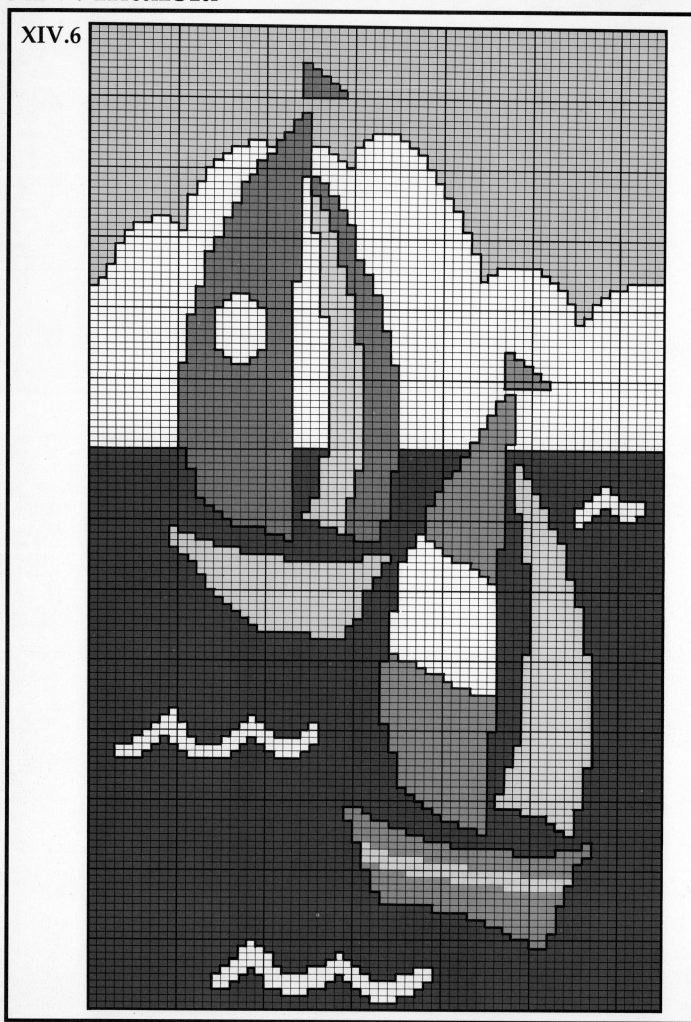

XIV. Intarsia

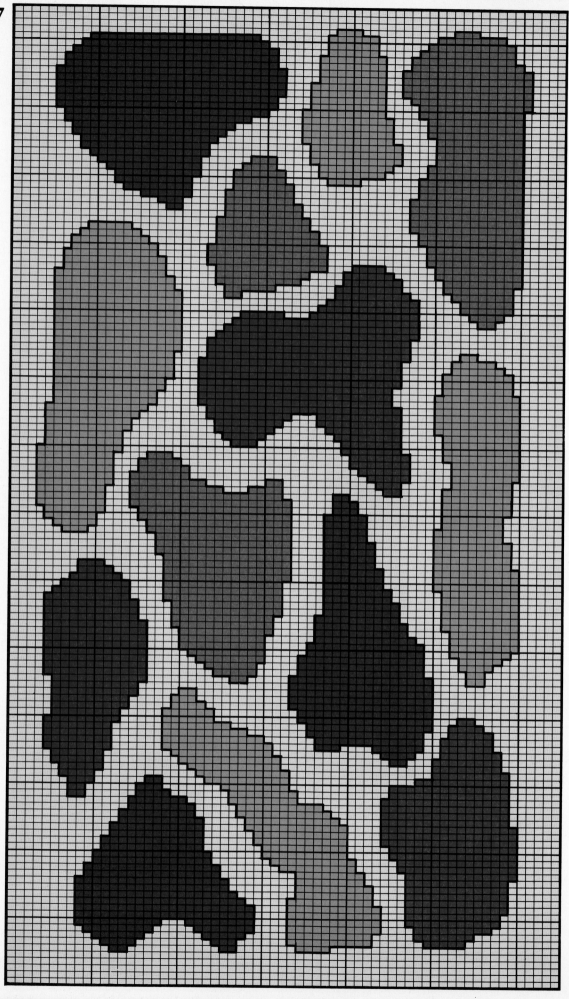

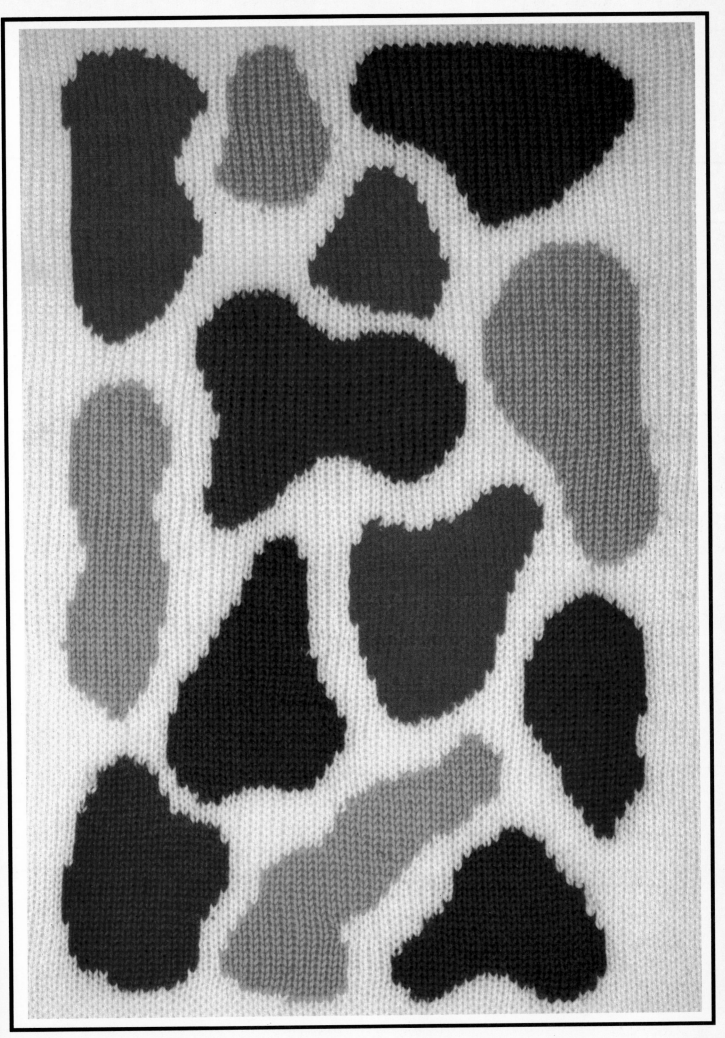

XIV. Intarsia

XIV.8

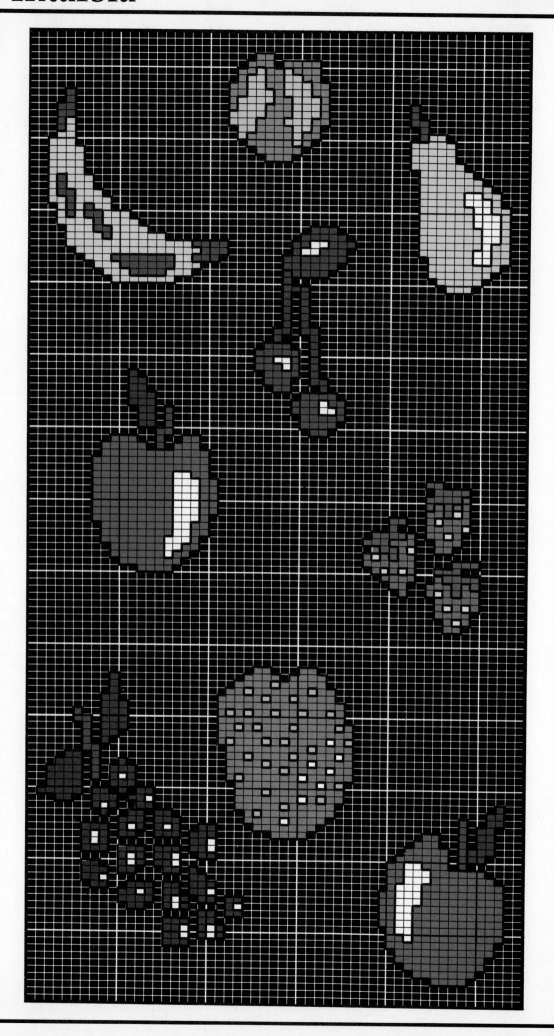

XIV. Intarsia

XIV. Intarsia

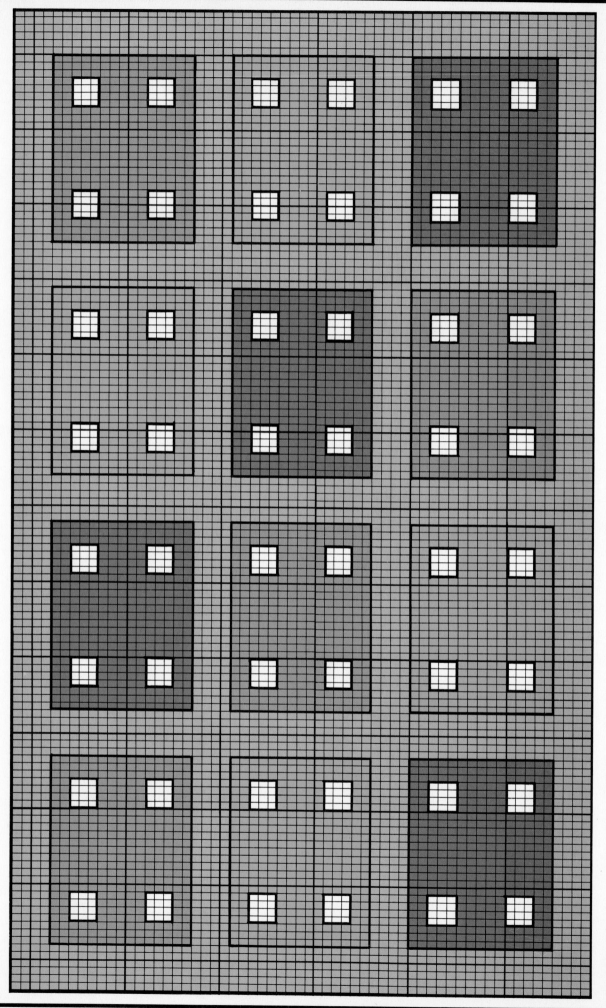

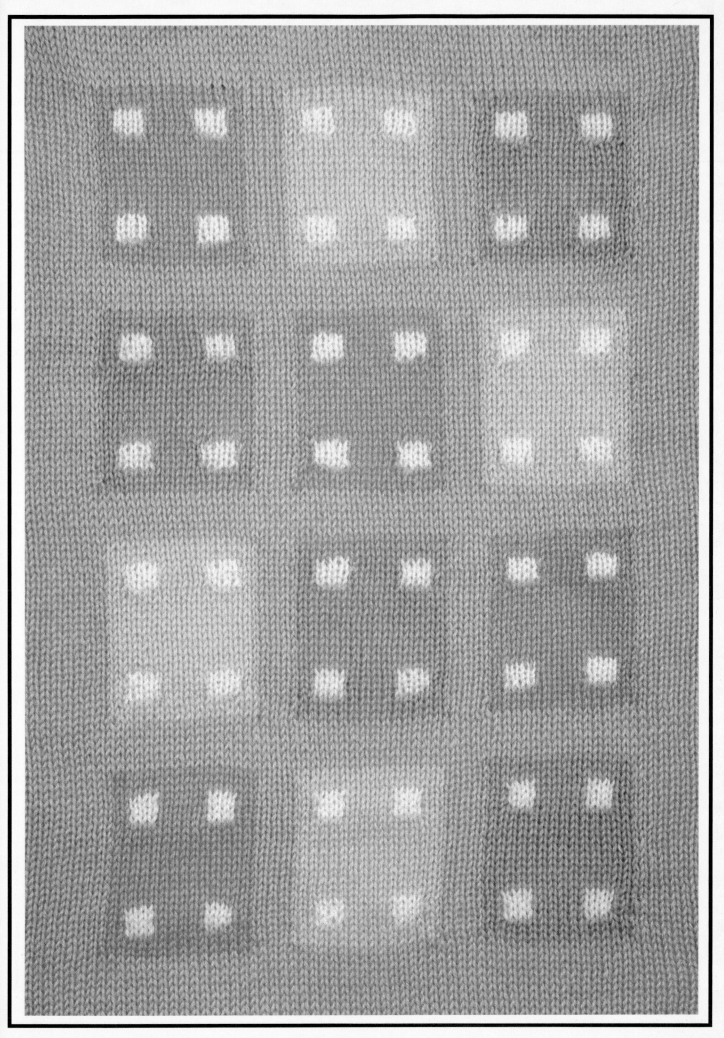

XIV. Intarsia

XIV.11

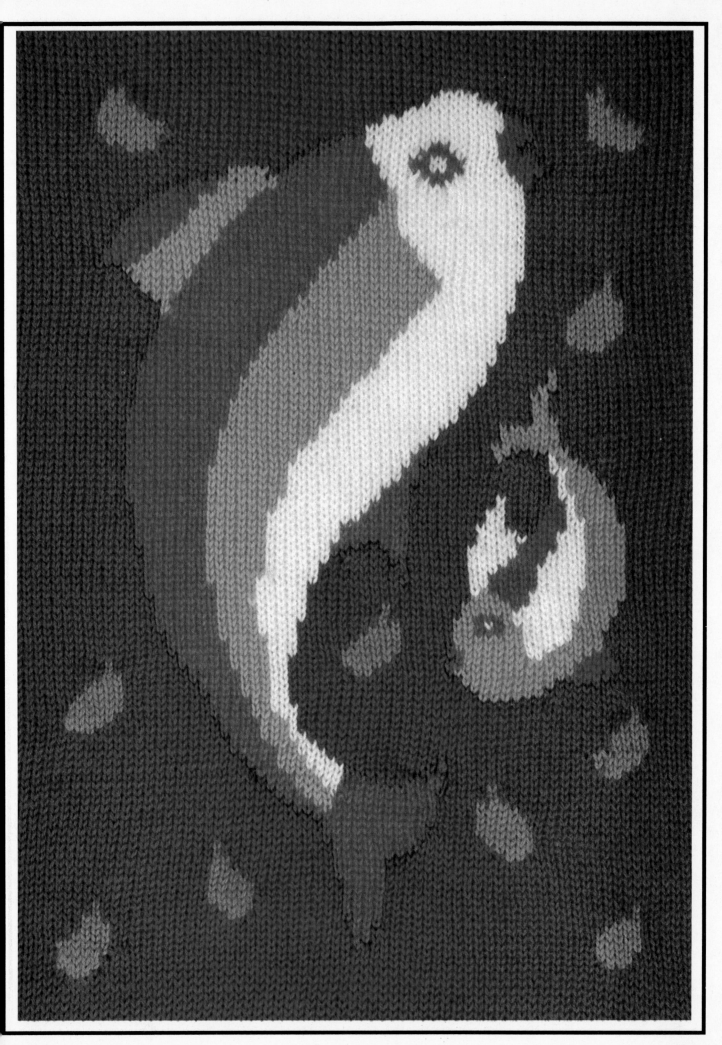

XIV. Intarsia

XIV.12